MW00943707

Editing by Jen Liddy
www.JenLiddy.com

Book Design by Sarah Ashmus Design
www.SarahAshmusDesign.com

ON THE
OTHER
SIDE

Messages From Spirit For Women

D R .   P A M   D E N T O N

SECTION 1

WHERE IT ALL BEGAN

I Am A Spiritual Messenger

*"Your life is a magical gift given to
you through source power."*

Love, Spirit

Straddling Two Worlds

How did I become a Medium?
How are these messages channeled?
When did I wake up to my gifts?
Why Female Leadership?

The Beginning of Connection

My Childhood

I sit and pray in my small bedroom, alone, lost, and searching, with only my teddy bear and books keeping me company.

The room itself is not scary: light and bright with blue flowery wallpaper, a blue bedspread, and soft pillow, it's a comfort to me. From my perch on the bed, I can see out of two windows. Out the window to my right is the 30-acre expanse of wooded land where we live. The light always comes through that window, and I know there is an angelic presence with me. I feel safe and warm connected to the land.

Out the other window is the coolest small zone of pine trees – my sanctuary. It is a magical land into which I escape any time I want, where I play in the wet moss and stones. This dark-wooded fairy-land is where I talk to the fairies in the grove. The faeries or *spirits of the woods* bring me joy and happiness.

When my life gets dark, stagnant, and lonely, I always have the magical fairy-land and the angelic open escape. I desperately need both escapes because fear is part of the daily landscape of my family life.

I do not know that I have intuitive powers or psychic capabilities. Intuition is merely part of my interior life, one that I share with no one.

My parents have such differing viewpoints on life, which leads to differing viewpoints on parenting. My dad has very strong ideas about who I should be and what I should do, while my mom is a very close, loving, but controlling force.

My parents' opposing energies and forces confuse me. When I get comfortable with my mother's smothering love, my dad changes it.

There is no structured, authentic conversation about who I am, what I am like, or what I want to be in the world. There is no consistent direction. During troubling times, I go into my room and talk to spirit...closing the door to pray.

I constantly escape into my imagination and the woods, to nurture myself, to soothe my psyche.

When I look back on that time, I wonder what I talked to my parents about. Did anyone ever hear me? Did I ever say, "I need help!"?

Living in the country, we were very isolated, so I was neither distracted from my experiences by friends, nor was I talking about it with other children. Of course, all I wanted was to be like everyone else. I wanted to live in a neighborhood, to play and run and stay out until the streetlights came on. I just wanted to be normal.

From the outside, it looked like we had it all together. In fact, I mastered the art of creating and showing Perfect Pam.

But I felt so abnormal and depressed.

And the many chaotic, controlling forces (including extended family) led to power struggles that made me feel like I was living a perfect life but would get caught on barbed wire if I said the wrong thing.

Hidden fears. Controlling attitudes of right and wrong. Opinions about how one should act. Polite manners. Limited freedom of expression. Unexpressed emotions.

These were the norms of my everyday life.

I wanted to ask, "Why can't I say what I am really thinking!? Why can't we express ourselves!?"

There was no pathway for truth and expression or feeling. The spiritual messages were coming in, but they had nowhere to go.

I was an intuitive picking up on everything in my environment. I was sensitive to the activity and chaos on the rural bus – with kids who came from the country. I was often depressed and shut down by age 10, because as an intuitive none of it made any practical sense. Life seemed so strange, constricted and contrived.

I didn't share my thoughts, experiences, or feelings with anyone, and the only person who had an inkling I was deep into my head with something was my mom. Though she said I was "special" and thought there "was something going on with Pammy", she just let me be and tried to support me in her motherly way. She taught me to work it out on my own. She used unconditional love and support from a distance.

But I wish someone had noticed that I had a special light. That I needed a channel for my interests, gifts, and intelligence. And though she knew I was special, my mom didn't have any tools to help me – other than taking me to church.

She thought that a church experience would facilitate my gifts in the world, making me feel spiritual and close to God.

But on that bed in the blue wallpapered room, I had the magic on the land, the connection to the spirits in the woods, and the bible. I used that bible to make sure I was "correctly" connecting to God. But by age 10, I knew it wasn't working.

I shut down and got lost in emotional pain, pissed off at the world because it didn't 'get' me.

I didn't have a place in this world. I looked at the other kids and realized they didn't feel the same things I was feeling. They were just living their lives: no burden of higher consciousness, no need to know what's going on.

What I didn't know at the time was that information was being shared *through me*. A kind of cosmic information flowed through me. And I was picking up on everything, sensitive to my environment. I had no idea this was detrimental because I lacked barriers to protect myself, nor did I have anyone to share this with!

Those other kids were *so free*. But they didn't get me, so I just had to shut up, learn to fit in the best I could, and create my own quiet relationship with God.

It was quite natural to me: my family was aligned with religion. And even though we didn't pray as a family, I called these moments talking to God. I'd ask for His guidance, support, and emotional healing. I was a "good Christian girl" who went to Baptist church on Sunday and sang in the choir.

But I didn't like church: it was cold and the message was dry. I never felt like I had direct access to God there. However, in my room, where I could channel, I felt safe – and that I could speak to God on my own terms.

Channeling was me opening through my body and head to reach out to God. I had no idea what I was doing, but I now know that I was opening what are my upper chakras, and I'd ask God for help.

My conscious memories of doing this start at ages 6 or 7.

My mom said she'd come into my room while I was sleeping only to find me upright, sleeping. Probably in my dream state I could get closer to spiritual energy. I recall white light and feeling peaceful, like a cylinder of energy descending around me so I could access vibrations of higher consciousness. I would sleepwalk, wandering, searching for spirit in the house, is my best guess.

Though I never felt afraid of the higher light (which I called God at the time), I was always terrified what was under the bed. Essentially, I was scared of the things with lower vibrational energies (ghosts, things hiding in my closet, demons, etc.) that I knew were there. Somehow I knew to look for them and tell them to go away, which they always did. I realize now many children don't know to tell them to disappear, but for some reason I had complete control and could shoo them away on my own.

But all of this wasn't meaningful to me because there seemed to be no place for me in the real world – except for my singular spiritual communion. I shut down enormously by the time I was 14, even though I kept up a good exterior with good grades, good friends, good behavior.

I followed the rules and tried to do the right thing, but inside I was turning judgment, hatred, and anger against my body. I started to turn myself against who I was becoming as a woman, and because I couldn't shine my light in an authentic way, it became self-hatred.

To compensate for this self-hatred, I became incredibly social.

As a good student of what was coming through via Spirit, I struggled with my earthly desire to be human and like everyone else. It was hard to not get on the bus and say something weird. Whenever my school friends would say something very human, I would counter with something that was "woo-woo" like, "Have you eaten your roughage today to make sure you're healthy?"

My Prayer:

Please help me feel better.
Please help me feel safe.
Please help me find love.
Please show me the way.

I was weird and wild, but people liked me anyway.

As I got older, I became a party girl, pushing all my energy toward seeking joy, happiness, and freedom with my amazing friends. We'd laugh, go swimming at night, take out boats on the lake. I craved any physical activity: biking, swimming, hiking in the woods. I'd rather have physical freedom with a lot of pain inside rather than be at home in my head with my spirituality.

When I could express myself as Party Pam with fun and happiness, I found that I was authentic. I could funnel my positive energy into social situations, bringing people together, and congregating in community. I learned that in community, if you're positive, functioning as a team and bringing each other up, life is an incredible ride.

I had the ability to feel what other people were feeling: when my friends were in trouble, when something was happening socially and I hadn't been included, where the next party was. I could see where people were gathering, who was there, and sense the differentiation between the many groups I engaged with.

I intuited my world based on other people's emotional status, spending hours watching them, their movements, postures, and attitudes.

Every job I had was about watching performance, then teaching it. Watch skiing, then teach it. Watch swimming, then teach it. I loved doing this because it kept my brain happy. I realized I could read people, sense their feeling, know where they'd been, understand what they struggle with.

During this time in my life, I realize I brought people together as a partier than as a light-giving spiritualist. And what I realize is that no matter whether I was Party Pam or the spiritual connector I am now and I was always a leader. I knew how to insert myself in a situation, make friends and allies, participate, yet never be part of the crowd.

That allowed me to pull myself out, insert myself into a different crowd, and repeat the pattern.

I see now that this was a co-dependent part of me. I wanted people to show me they loved me, while at the same time I was never able to stay in one place or allow anyone to get close to me.

Figuring out how to be "human enough" to interact with people was important – I needed love, companionship, acceptance, adventure, activity, like everyone else! I quickly learned to straddle both worlds – Spirit and Earthly, so I could be surrounded by a strong community.

It wasn't until years later that I understood that navigating varied groups and worlds was part of my training to be the adult I am today. But during this time, I was confused and alienated by it. I never allowed myself to get too close to people.

Now I know because it's when you're a medium, a conduit of information, it's vital to not be attached to the messages and junk that comes through.

This straddling is a blessing and curse: I still work very hard to cultivate a community of "my people", those who understand my woo-woo side while living in a very 3-dimensional, secular world with judgment, pain and money. The people who I surround myself with enjoy my spiritual side: they find it entertaining and call on it when they need it.

I want intimacy: sometimes I want to be stuck in my human form, snuggling up to people and getting close to them. But I know now that my role is to transmit information, flowing through it and moving on. Spiritualists cannot attach to it, or else the energies come into your body. They are not yours: they block clarity and create health problems. A medium or spiritualist cannot do her job if her channel is blocked or clogged. I closed my channel with Party Pam, but she created an amazing skill for me: creating spiritual community. If not for her, I would've been a lone wolf, living among the fairies in the woods.

A lot has happened since my childhood and adolescence. And I have been led by spirit to open up and receive messages that will help people, especially women, heal their lives.

I have dedicated my life to spiritual messaging for clients and practitioners. Within this book, you'll explore what leadership looks like *On the Other Side*, with spirit designed for women. You will learn how to pass through the wall of stuck and sabotage to get to the true form of your leadership. You'll likely come to realize that we need Female Leadership programs in our schools, in our businesses, in our families. That it's not just a 'woman issue', it is an everybody issue: every person must accept life change as immediate and necessary.

You'll be asked to work on your relationship with yourself, strengthening your positive attributes and beliefs in yourself, then beginning to strengthen your relationship with the world around you. Maybe that's a small community like your family or a large one like a business or institution. It could be your health, your relationships, or your family.

You'll explore who you are as a person, emerge your quality of authentic heart-centered leadership, and bring out the real woman inside of you by fast forwarding through your stuck.

Finally, you'll learn to help others, old and young, to realize who they are outside of their home that we all have an authentic purpose, that we are not the roles/norms that may have been established at home. We draw things from our family that are important to who we are – but *they don't define who we are now*.

It doesn't matter what you do or who you are as a woman or man: *you have feminine leadership qualities and abilities inside of you.*

You have heart centered leadership inside of you. You have guidance from spirit. This book is designed to help you access those.

Each message is special and unique. It's up to you how and whether you apply them.

How To Use The Spiritual Messages

My spiritual powers awakened fully when I was working as a Chiropractor. As I navigated the world, I was guided to different experiences and lessons that would heighten my awareness, opening me to channel intuitively. Throughout my many years as a healer, medium and spiritual guide, I have been asked by women to repeat the messages over and over.

There is something about the way that they are communicated that has helped my clients feel at ease and awaken to peaceful inner *knowing*.

The messages I share with you in *On the Other Side* are derived from the information that appeared repetitively in my healing practice.

I want to share these messages and insights with you because, across the board for women, these messages are very important. Essentially, the messages are information that has been *missing from your life*. And, when applied, they help you heal your life, reclaim your power, and open you to understand who you are crafted to become as a female leader.

Each message is different, carrying threads of repetitive messaging and language.

The repetitive reinforcement of messaging helps you heal and can empower how you live your daily life.

As you work through your stuck and sabotage, understand that we all have blocks that need to be addressed and removed.

Write

Many of the messages have transformation exercises and questions that I recommend you write about and explore. Writing is subconscious and provides intuitive processing that will help move you into life change. Have a journal or notebook ready as you read to help capture your thoughts as they come through and facilitate your personal process of empowering your authentic purpose.

SECTION 2

YOU
HAVE A
CALLING

Your Destiny Is Calling You

"We want you to know how amazing you are <u>right now</u> so that you can gather the power to move to the other side and lead from your intuition. Your intuition knows why you are here, your intuition knows your destiny, and your intuition can create your connection to purpose."

Love, Spirit

I know inside my heart that every woman has a purpose, a reason for being here on earth, a destiny, and a calling. Spirit has guided me over and over to help women open their destiny and connect to purpose.

Spirit has also shown me that inside every woman is a divine spark of *creative spiritual destiny* designed especially for her own contribution to the world.

As a medium, healer, and business leader, I have learned first-hand that women around the world are putting out their divine spark daily. Some women do not even know they have power.

From channeling messages from spirit over and over, I believe there is the other side to our lives as women, a side that most of us have not seen or experienced. It is the intuitively-driven and spiritually inspired part of life that I like to call the Female Form of Leadership.

On the Other Side: Messages from Spirit for Women will help you make connections that open you to your amazing power and spiritual truth. On the other side of what we are currently experiencing – negativity, pain, suffering, sickness, lack, darkness, sexual shut-down and struggle – is our purpose and reason for being here on earth. As we look to the other side we will awaken to the life we truly desire.

The Spiritual Push

My spiritual messages have guided me to realize it is time to wake up our 'woo-woo' and get to spiritual work! And connect directly to intuition.

The call for women's spiritual awakening is urgent, mandatory and pushed by spirit through our 'awake' leaders. The earth needs our intuitive and visionary strength. We are in a red zone and cannot wait any longer to connect and communicate with spirit – and ourselves.

Message From Spirit

To get to the other side we must acknowledge that women have walls - blocks, sabotage, and 'stuck-ness' that hold us back from a new perception. Our blocks have become a governing pattern we must deal with head-on. Therefore, Female Leadership – our REAL leadership – requires vulnerability, transparency, and authentic emotion.

To Women

To ignite a bigger picture of world change, a new form of Female Leadership must emerge and women like you are key to getting this job done. Hidden deep within every woman's soul is Female Leadership that must be uncovered, excavated, and recognized to restore balance to the world.

Our female form of leadership is on the other side of our daily story and our daily struggles. It requires an absolute FLIP of our daily reality. And it takes spirit, faith and guidance because our leadership is so radically different from what we are currently experiencing in the patriarchy.

Guidance Has Shown Me

Know that each of us has a real, authentic, and important reason for being here – and to access our purpose our walls must come down.

To cultivate power, women need to take an inward journey to discover what makes us powerful. Our success cannot be spoon-fed, told, or delivered to us by the outside world. We must go inward and create a belief system that tunes us into our ultimate power and true potential – our innate feminine wisdom.

We cannot be told to be powerful.

We have to BE powerful.

And this process requires women to move beyond the old stories holding us back and engage in our destined truth.

I am not talking about small scale change. I'm talking about huge surges of feminine power on the planet that say to the masculine energy we mean BUSINESS.

We are here to make change happen.

That we are here to create balance and restore communication between matriarchy and patriarchy.

That we will not back down when the patriarchy resists our presence. As many women wake up to working within a man's world, I want Female Leadership empowerment to awaken men to the value of having women on their team.

What About The Men

We can get to a place where we want men to love and respect our work just as we have supported them for thousands of years. I want men and women to see the value of collaborating to create a more balanced version of leadership.

And the only way to do this is if women rise up and fully claim our right to lead, sharing our abilities with the patriarchy in a firm and direct way.

Defining Feminine Leadership

*"Women have a unique form of intelligence that must
be uncovered, revealed, and respected in order for the
world to change. It is buried deep within your souls
and you must excavate it <u>now</u>."*

Love, Spirit

Exactly what do I mean by 'Female Leadership'? Maybe you're thinking of the masculine model of credentials, title, position, hierarchy, linear thinking, practical thought, analysis, big deals and emotionless energy. This is natural because women have been trained to do business and live life within the masculine form of leadership.

Women, however, are the real, transparent, raw and vulnerable deal – we are not cookie cutter, Barbie doll, robotic or perfect for that matter. We are the creative life force on the planet. We vision, create and support humanity.

Why?

Because we are a natural resource of creative and community power. We function best when we have space to express ourselves in a real and authentic way. Yet, for most of us, this is nearly impossible because we are still trying so hard to be good and do the right thing to please the established masculine model.

Many women have had to shut up, put up, play the game, and step into the masculine arena to make it. But playing the game has meant a huge sacrifice of our health and happiness. We have had to stiffen up, toughen up, play by the rules and put on a happy face. We have had to endure being put down, shut out, put upon and downgraded.

In our pleasing status, we have tuned out, shut down, and dried up. We do things for outside acceptance rather than listening to our inner knowing.

And this avoidance is programmed so deeply into our daily code of operations that we naturally over look the OTHER side.

Let's change this story! In my countless hours of dedicated work toward women's empowerment and channeling spiritual messages, I've learned we all have a leadership style that is innate to our feminine power.

Feminine Intelligence

We are **intuitive,** with natural feelings that guide us that we must honor and acknowledge as real.

We are **creators**, knowing how to manifest and create change.

We are **community-builders**, thriving when we collaborate with others.

Yet we currently live the opposite way, turning against ourselves (via self-criticism) and against each other (via catty backstabbing). Many women follow the boy's club rule book without even knowing we are doing it, yet we yearn for more because these rules go against our true nature.

On the Other Side guides you to switch this paradigm and retrieve the intuitive power you may not know you have or that you may have depleted along the way. You will pull to the surface your innate feminine power – the things that are divinely yours already. Within the pages of this book are messages and a path to help you to receive your real greatness.

Message from Spirit

EMERGE!
*Every woman has a leader inside her waiting
to emerge. But for many years we have created
blocks, obstacles, and sabotage which keep
us from emerging in our full power.*

This book serves to explain why this is a real societal and world problem.

And it is my soul purpose to use my intuitive wisdom to help you – and all women – unlock our amazing gifts of authentic leadership and fully express our true selves. I want women to move beyond lack and stuck, taking up space and living a vital life. I want more money to flow through the hands of female businesses. I want women to be empowered by intuition. I want you to listen to higher guidance and KNOW you are amazing.

As a spiritual guide and medium, I help people get in touch with the messages that our body's spirit shares with us. Our bodies, wired through the nervous system to provide spiritual guidance, inform us of why we're here. Every-body has the same wiring to spirit and guidance from the universe.

We call this the Higher Self.

The spiritual guidance is provided through sensation, positive feelings, messages, intuition, and spiritual communication. Our nervous system is *designed* to release and reorganize tension and old patterns, improving and changing our quality of life. And it is designed to receive source power.

Our nervous system continually connects us to the spiritual messages that help us access guidance. But! This incredible design has been thwarted and distorted by our ingrained patterns of self-limiting beliefs, emotional baggage, and walls of steel. It has built patterns that BLOCK the other side from communicating directly with our senses.

Our innate inner intelligence is our divine birthright – our destiny – and is what makes us powerful. Accessing it is how we act on purpose and live a fulfilled, happy, and healthy life!

However, in practice as a spiritual guide, I see people turn off, shut down, or block their innate intelligence – to a devastating effect. Useless information is pumped into people every day – I call them 'black blobs of negativity' and negative interference. And the negativity becomes sludge in our nervous system, blocking the Higher Self from communicating effectively.

This low-vibrational negative interference manifests as fear, sabotage, and stuck energy. It keeps our spiritual guidance out. The low vibration creates ugly behaviors, greed, meanness, hatred, pain, suffering, and disease.

My Story

Initially, when I began my intuitive career as a Chiropractor, my job was to release the stress and tension of a burdened nervous system.
This would open up life force, i.e. the flow of this innate intelligence.

And as I practiced this on my patients, my own ability to communicate with spirit and higher guidance stepped in to lead the way. I quickly realized I wanted to use my 6th sense to help people connect and communicate to their *real reason for being on earth*, which is NOT to live with negativity and pain!

Along my path as a Chiropractic Physician working with the physical body – and later as a Medium – I learned that women specifically have a Feminine Intelligence, an inner knowing of what we want out of life.

Women were drawn intuitively to find out why they are here more so than the men I'd see in my practice. Why? Because women's natural flow of intuitive energy has creative power, links us to our desires, and creates purposeful momentum.

But I also realized we as women are not in touch with our overall health, our innate intelligence, *and most certainly not* our feminine intelligence. The women I saw were not connected to spirit, but they had a huge yearning to GET CONNECTED. They just didn't know how – nor did they know why it was so hard for them.

Here's the why: major disturbances and interferences block our spirit, mostly because we live in our head, not in the natural flow of feminine energy and intuition. What blocks us? Too much intellect! This is so hard to digest, but the imbalance lives between our intuition (feeling) and our thinking. Our thoughts are absolutely in the way of our feelings. And this keeps women stuck.

So how does a woman tap into her Higher Self? And wire Higher Self to her power and flow of feminine intelligent energy?

This book is designed to help you see the path of "how". And the good news is that, when tapped, intelligent feminine energy becomes a natural extension or expression of a woman's authentic personality. Her spirit and energy guides a woman to stand strong in the face of masculine challenges. She can then remain true to her desires, destiny, and purpose.

You are that woman. You can access your innate, feminine intelligence – once you get past your blocks.

Women Are Holding Back

"It's NOT your fault! Past programming is holding you back from traversing to the next phase of abundant living. In order to make it to the other side you will need to recognize the generational stressors that contribute to your stuck energy and learn to release what no longer belongs to you."

Love, Spirit

"What holds you back? Why have you hesitated for so long to step up and lead? Why do you reject the mere idea of leadership?"

Spirit wants us to look at these questions and thoughts.

Let's examine blocks, because though our path is open and we are unfolding our female intuitive intelligence, the kickback of our past programming is a huge challenge.

(PS: Even women perceived as 'leading the way' exhibit sabotaging patterns and are subject to the black blobs of negative interference that block their paths, too! Most women are stressed out to the max!)

So often women have shared with me that they are sick, stuck, unhappy, depressed, anxious, guilty, filled with worry and doubt, playing small, not leading at all, or hiding. Yet they want more out of life. Women share that they just CAN NOT get out of their own way to become an amazing success. Usually it's an issue of *lack*: lack of time, lack of money, lack of energy, and lack of motivation.

Why?! Why are we sabotaging ourselves? Why are we stuck?

It is not your fault!

Message From Spirit

Spirit has shown me that our blocks are real. There are blocks on our feminine leadership that we must remove to access real abundance. These blocks are encoded in our minds and bodies, passed on to us as generational stressors. Unless we shift the stress, success will continue to elude us, remaining a dream - not a reality.

Spirit has also shown me that these blocks can be removed.

Take a look at programming through Feminism.

Feminism paved the way for women to step out into the workforce, put on a suit and tie, and 'man up'. But it did not at all give us equal respect, pay, or rights. The women who have come before us paved the way to 'equality' but we have not made it yet. We are not fulfilled or in balance. And we are not working together with men and respected.

Statistics show that women – more than ever – are in pain, suffering, sick, under paid, raped, shoved in a box, turned off, tuned out, and stifled. This is a huge problem, and it is not just an American problem: it is *global*.

Many women are searching for ways to wake up now because they see the problem and hear the call.

What do women lack? What are women missing? Why are we still not leading?

The vast majority of us lack access to our feminine *star power*: confidence. Access to confidence means we are willing to shine *no matter what*! And I really mean NO MATTER WHAT! To speak up NO. MATTER. WHAT.

The only way to access this confidence, this feminine star power of our destiny, is to dig deep, break through the generational stress, and stand up for what we believe is right, from the base up and from spirit down.

We must discover what we are amazing at doing and focus on getting *that* out into the world.

And the most effective place – the only place – to do this work is in sisterhood, in community, in relationship with other women. And do it with spiritual guidance, love and support.

In many cases the shutdown of the female leader and feminine intelligence has been so extreme that women are not even *aware* they have a *choice* to access greatness. They don't even know they can rise to the top of their life, business or industry!

Many women still feel that the way we are living is "ok," "fine", and "good." That we need to cover up and shut up who we really are and hide from the world.

This has become women's emotional reality.

The "I am fine" status causes a shutdown of our feminine power and has been ingrained in us by the external subliminal messages we receive from the world we live in today, a world that has been set up to operate on masculine principles.

It does not serve our inner female power or celebrate outward female success. These principles reward efficiency over equality, the end product versus the effort, a 'no pain no gain' ideology, and the bottom line instead of true rewards. The big is celebrated over the small and the external celebrated over the internal.

Yet there are things that women do every day that *have to be* acknowledged and celebrated!

We are the creators of the planet. We manifest life. And our simple act of being female is the power that can set women free from lack. Feminine intelligence keeps the world going, and we deserve to acknowledge our **brilliance and genius**.

The world as we know it, in many cases, does not take into account alternate methods to accomplish the similar goals that come more naturally to women. It is my assertion that these methods are valid and *must* be embraced! Women have a valuable and real contribution to the business world, institutions, and politics. *Feminine intelligence* needs to be expressed, respected, and honored.

And it starts with you.

Message From Spirit

You are Key to Change. We need you. Empowerment to Female Leadership is a process, an unfolding toward resolution of blocks and sabotage. This is our way to the top of our life. When you feel like you want to back out from the process, know that it is because you are close to resolving deep internal conflict, releasing generational stress and that this is the time to stay in it, to be in sisterhood!

For many women, the desire to move forward can be thwarted by an inner voice that tells us we are crazy to try, that we are not good enough for a myriad of reasons, that success in business, love, and money can't possibly be ours. I promise, *we will tackle these voices of dissent later.*

Let the feminine path unfold as you work through the truth in *On the Other Side.* Your program for ultimate success is innate, internal, and natural. It is encoded wisdom in you, driven by the natural state of *feminine intuition, creation,* and *community-building.*

Fear might grip you as you're required to resolve deep painful issues, but as long as you follow the exercises in the book, you will have a direct pipeline into the female wisdom and connection you need to continue *your* process in a positive way.

We are going to build a feminine model of leadership that includes *your* voice and calling. This model is collaborative, community based, win-win, intuitive, vulnerable, transparent, nurturing, natural, unfolding, flowing, connecting, creative, open, allowing, pleasure filled, abundant, and supportive.

The model you'll receive here will facilitate your expression of self- and star-powers; it will **not** hold you back from your greatness. There will be times in this journey that seem impossible, but trust me: it *can* be done, and the fastest path there is to build support for your leadership evolution through inner study.

Before moving on let's examine your generational patterns. Accept them as real blocks. And apply the polarity exercise to look at the other side of your story. Flip it!

Journaling Exercise:

What generational stressors do you know you carry?

What holds you back that your female friends, mom, grandmothers, or other women have passed along?

Can you identify any self-limiting phrases that you use over and over? For example, "No pain, no gain". "Fight your way to the top". "Only in a man's world".

Now rewrite this story, FLIP the context.

Here's how: What have you gained from women around you? If nothing comes to you make sure to flip one of the negative statements and rewrite it into a statement of positive guidance. Write these positive statements down.

You may also choose to applaud feminism.

What do you feel the leading feminists and success driven women have contributed to your life?

Learn To Play Big

"Women by birthright are the change makers, the trend-setters, and the decision makers. Women are real creators and visionaries. We want you to hold a positive vision for the progress of humanity."

Love, Spirit

On the Other Side is for women who want to access leadership in a new way and build a stronger foundation for enjoying life and accessing what they truly want and deserve. It is for life-changers, consciousness-raisers and those who want to be 'out of the box' thinkers.

Truly, it is for those who feel boxed in and feel there must be way more to life than just sitting in a cube. Maybe you want to live life from a more expansive place. Maybe you believe in more possibility. And maybe you want to achieve more access to life change.

You don't want to buy into fear-based living or control. You want more out of life and are willing to do what it takes to access the changes you seek.

This process of spiritual awakening is for women who want to tune into purpose, finding their calling to live a largely expansive life – outside of the box. Most of all, it's for those who feel that it's time for women to emerge as leaders and lead in our own feminine way.

Why did I call this book *On the Other Side*? Because I was guided that women must look to the other side of our stuck and sabotage to find their Inner Strength, become leaders, and activate on the ideas inside of us! Big Ideas!

I know you have a project inside of you that is valuable, money-generating, and powerful. Your idea is inside of you, waiting to be born, monetized, and built into a powerful structure of purpose, business, and leadership. Use the tools above to move past stuck. Move into your creative glory and abundance. Use community to support you, instead of suffering in silence?

I don't know the details of your life, but I do know you have a hidden power to Play Big. And this expansion of your Inner Knowing helps heal the blocks you are facing. I want you to own your space, hold the space, and create the space for you to Play Big.

Message From Spirit

*Do not buy into fear-based living or control.
We know you want more out of life and are
willing to do what it takes to access the changes
you seek. You have a burning desire inside of you
and it is time to unleash your star power. You can
tune into purpose, find your calling and live a
largely expansive life – outside of the box. Most of
all, you can feel your own feminine way.*

Become bigger in your success than you ever imagined possible. Grow and expand. It is inside of you.

If something inside of you wonders, "Is this relevant to me? Can I apply this to my particular needs? Am I a leader? *Do I deserve to Play Big as a leader?*"

I want to shout, Yes. Yes. Yes! Spirit wants to shout YESSSSSSS!

Keep reading! You will come to understand the programming blocking us from stepping forward. When you know the block, you can go through it. It's that easy.

Recognize the block. Make a decision to get unblocked. Then I will show you how to channel the spirit of change.

The Mental Shift To Playing Big

To get to the other side of your challenges and pain, let's talk about Play Big Mind Set.

Inner Strength is about standing up for your truth and inner knowing of what you want. While developing inner strength one of the biggest challenges you will encounter is staying small.

In this book Play Big refers to breaking patterns that hold you stuck and in a small position. Women, in particular, are taught to "play small" at a very young age: hold back, hide our feelings, not be heard, not share the truth, fit in, and not stand out. "Be the same and fit in" is the message we hear repeatedly.

Women are taught to apologize for our mere presence on the earth, say *I'm sorry* and make excuses for ourselves, our words, our thoughts, our actions. When we're taught this, when these are the expectations for us, how can we ever Play Big and make an impact in the world?

All we're doing is running programs and stories, holding patterns imprinted into us as children, passed along through generations of training. Notice how many times we say, "I'm sorry" when there is no cause to apologize! We apologize for taking up space.

We are brought up as girls to hold back. Not speak up. Be quiet. And stay small.

And truthfully, I know you'll stay small when I let you. I say this not with judgment or criticism, but instead because women are TRAINED to be small. Only a few figure out how to run with the big dogs and Play Big.

So what does that mean, and why have I chosen this language?

First, know that when I say Play Big, I know you may already vote yourself off the show as an inconsequential player! Like, you don't matter. "There are only a few BIG players. How could I ever be one?"

1%, 1 person at the top, 1 team wins.

Think again!

In this case...

You deserve more! You are already more than you know!

When we Play Big we move beyond the stuck, stagnant, small self into the alive, expressive power that is our birthright. We override sabotaging behaviors that hold us down and keep us sick, stuck, unhappy, ineffective. It transitions us into a person who tunes in to inner reality of truth. Life changes for the better: we want and actually get it.

As you engage with spirit you will start to dive into the *thought* of being bigger energetically, emotionally, spiritually, and professionally.

You will begin to take up space in the world, speak your truth, stand in your power, feel your Inner Strength. Play Big to experience worthiness, self-love, respect, and purpose. Share your voice, be heard, and take care of yourself first.

Playing big allows women to use our creative powers and resources to heal ourselves and our families, build strong businesses, and lead with confidence.

Why I Chose To Play Big And Go To The Other Side Of The Story

Why would I want to break these patterns and become a female leader? Why would I want to do this difficult work?

I know in my heart that every person has a calling, a reason for being here on earth to make an impact. I woke up to my own personal calling as a young woman in college. Depression drove me to seek something bigger, better, and more powerful.

From deep dark depression, I emerged as a light-work leader, finding my way out of the darkness by seeking alternative sources of spiritual support and healing. I discovered inside of my soul was a spirit waiting to wake up and emerge in love and joy. I've been working on emerging my female power for over 20 years, but luckily you won't have to take this long because what I have discovered is a path to override the stuck!

My inner voice of truth told me to stop playing small. It was time to realize my true potential. I was called out of the darkness into a spiritual path of transformation. And in order to transmute what I like to call my black blobs of deep soul pain, negative interference and feminine hardship, I had to become a master of my own spiritual universe...and *lead*.

I had no road map or compass, so I learned to do this all my own, listening with my intuition and tuning in to the calling of my higher soul purpose. And I followed the guidance of a few trusted teachers.

At your disposal, you have a fast path beyond your obstacles – because the answers to your freedom are in the pages of this book.

Your Play Big begins with a calling, the inner knowing of a woman who is embracing purpose, choosing mission first, and leading from that mission. Let's redefine "play" from being on the floor with kids to the adult form of play: honing the creative powers that create our passion. Play is using our inner creativity and knowing to make the life that we want. It is leading from our mission and playing in our natural birthright of success.

But you must believe you deserve it.

That's a calling. When we are called, we feel passion. It's an inner surge of energy and a positive drive to do something bigger, to move outside the box we've created for ourselves (or the one that has been created for us!).

When called to Play Big, there is a sense of inspiration. There is a sense of spiritual guidance, whether you believe in that or not, because you are moved to step outside the box. You are moved to stop feeling constricted and limited. You are done with lack. You want more out of life. This is spirit moving you forward.

I call it 'living in our star power': it's the gift, the superpower, the calling that is *simply just what we are good at.*

- It's the woman who is a natural listener and <u>follows her calling</u> to provide therapy for another person.

- It's the woman who is a natural teacher and <u>follows her calling</u> to show people new paths and opportunities.

- It's the woman who is a natural organizer and <u>follows her calling</u> to provide help for people to focus and stay on track.

- It's the woman who is the natural intuitive and <u>follows her calling</u> to help people sense their lives beyond the physical realm.

- It's the woman who is collaborative and <u>wants to work together</u> to achieve a common goal.

Journaling Exercise:

Identify your gift.

- What's your gift? Don't know? Examine what you do in your free time!

- What are the things you enjoy doing?

- What brings you joy?

- What do you do that brings you fulfillment?

- What makes you feel alive and full of energetic flow?

- What comes naturally and is easy for you?

Describe yourself in detail.

Play Big Money And Success

*"We want you to let go of stress and pain. We want
you to learn how to step into the flow and be
abundant. You deserve this now."*

Love, Spirit

Look To *Your* Posture And Expressions Of Playing For Answers

If the opposite of being playful is being stressed, think of the stressed person's expressions: tight face, closed-off, hunched-over body, shut down heart, and fear-based posture. They're grouchy.

When someone is playing, they are relaxed, smiling, breathing deeply, open, and friendly. Their heart is beating and enriching the body with oxygen. They appear younger and stronger because they are empowered by spirit.

The analytical, grouchy mind wonders, "How can I possibly build a business through play? How can I get anything done? How absurd."

But remember, play is living on purpose with a lighter attitude and a belief in a positive outcome. Possibly, for the big players with a big mission, it's to create a positive outcome and impact for future generations.

Unfortunately, society has defined play as frivolous or competitive. Or that it's overly exciting, adventurous, or provides a high adrenaline rush. Sometimes violent or extremely physical, play often includes inflicting pain on other people and/or drinking and drugging.

Instead of focusing on the societal definitions of play, ask yourself, "What brings me laughter? What brings a smile to my face? What brings me peace and calm?"

Your answer will be authentic, real and honest.

Expressing your true self, whatever, however, and unhindered, allows you to take off the shackles so you can move and feel your authentic expression. *This is play.*

Taking these qualities and putting them into a leadership position is *Playing Big*. This is leading from a place of joy, abundance, and community. When we pursue these qualities professionally, we've found our calling.

How Jen Found Spirit Calling Her To Play Big

Jen ran a company that wasn't her purpose: it was someone else's big dream. It depleted and exhausted her. When she plugged into what made her feel 'playful', she realized though her 'play' wasn't typical, it did bring her joy, relaxation, and fulfillment.

What was it? Organizing. Helping others. Building people up. Teaching. Scheduling. Connecting. Writing. Showing people how to be accountable to get what they wanted.

"In the company I was running, I realized that my personality didn't fit into that structure. I felt constantly at war with what was going on there. So, I began to play, dabbling in my off-time passions."

What emerged was an accountability coaching company, working with people to help them achieve their goals, move out of their own way, and organize themselves. "I realized that organizing is like breathing to me. To get to teach people how to do this is not work. It's play that I get paid for!"

Gina is another example: she ran her husband's company but was fatigued, run down, and depressed doing it. However, she felt she had no choice. In her spare time, she honed the skills of energy working, which is her star power. She is gifted here, and it's her play. She began to draw to her clients that fulfill her. She found joy in her work and is getting paid for it! She is now a Spiritual Guide for women to access their inner healing power.

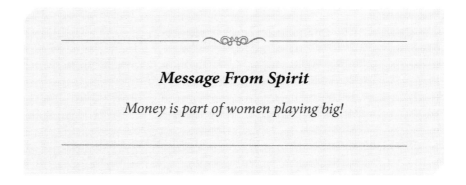

Message From Spirit

Money is part of women playing big!

Spirit has shown me that Play Big means *money*. Women have to Play Big with cash flow. I believe in monetizing a woman's purpose and making *big* money is a spiritual purpose.

Money has a spirit. Money has energy. Money can speak to you and guide you. Money is attached to everything we do as humans. You have a relationship with money.

On the opposing side, lack of money is also energetic and looking into the spiritual energy of lack can help you gain insight into your purpose.

Your big money attitude will be different than someone else's, as everyone needs or desires a different amount in life. The importance to money is that women step out of <u>lack</u> and into <u>abundance</u>. Spiritual guidance has shown me over and over that women are trapped in low thoughts about money and poverty. We feel limited and stuck when it comes to wealth.

The first step to abundance is through your leadership and destiny. It's in believing that the universe can work for you, rather than against you.

Playing Big involves fulfillment and financial success. A large part of the fulfillment of the Play Big strategy is to make sure we **monetize** our purpose – in other words, how can we get paid for the thing we're really good at?

Message From Spirit

Money must flow into the hands of heart-centered women, spiritualists, consciousness raisers, and rule benders. Don't give your gifts away, and don't downplay your gifts. Women tend to de-value their gifts because they come easily to them, and that is a huge mistake. This work is about giving value to our gifts in a way that contributes to change from the bottom up: starting with oneself, moving through the family, through the community, and into the world.

Play Big and bring power back to your leadership.

Begin To Be Real

To understand *On the Other Side* as an important life change and to Play Bigger than you ever imagined, we have to start with leadership – as it is today.

Where are we as leaders?
What do we believe as leaders?
Do we see ourselves as leaders?

Journaling Exercise:

- What does leadership mean to you, right now in this moment?

- How does the word leadership make you feel?

Journal on being real with the word leadership.

SHAPING YOUR LEADERSHIP

Women As Leaders

*"You are a leader and you must learn to
believe it and accept it!"*

Love, Spirit

To understand *On the Other Side* as an important life change and to Play Bigger than you ever imagined, we have to start with leadership – as it is today.

Where are women as leaders? What do women believe as leaders? Do women see themselves as leaders?

I've spent many years talking to people, especially women, about leadership and facilitating shifts in perception and life change all around leadership. The answers to "What do you think about leadership?" I get are tiring, analytical, and dry.

Many women I coach and talk to who already see themselves as leaders are boxed into an inauthentic, hierarchical, masculine, and exclusive structure. They think that leadership is a bad word, something to be avoided. And they are dried up in their purpose and calling. Life has become mundane and boring.

Women generally believe there are a few powerful leaders and all the rest are non-leaders. They think that leadership is dominating, aggressive, and controlling. 'Leadership' is a dirty word.

Leadership is perceived as an exclusive quality or role, not an inclusive one, and certainly not something that is within every single one of us.

By looking at leadership from the inside out and from a more female and *intuitive edge*, *On the Other Side* can help women transform how we move forward in life.

It's designed to deconstruct the hierarchy and make leadership – well – accessible to every woman.

And as you begin to gain awareness of hierarchy, you will also notice how it is totally ineffective. Hierarchy promotes control, fear, punishment, and conformity. Female Leadership promotes collaboration, love, self-worth, authenticity, transparency, and vulnerability.

Why did I choose Female Leadership as the catalyst of *On the Other Side*?

Here is the story.

My path to leadership and Play Big theory began in the early 2000s. I was a Chiropractor working with people's nervous systems. I clarify this because most people assume that Chiropractic care is for back pain only, and it is way more than that. We help the patient access life-force, the innate inner healing wisdom of the body.

Chiropractic is about the body's innate intelligence and ability to recognize what needs to be healed – and heal it or change it. It's our inner-healing system and how we relate to the world. It's turning on our power and tuning into awareness of energy and life-force.

In Chiropractic we ask the questions "What heals us? What drives us? How do we thrive instead of survive?"

And for me it was also about life-purpose and connection. I realized through adding spiritual studies and energy medicine, the nervous system is deeper than I thought. It's the gateway to awareness, self-correction, self-reflection and destiny. My work was about brain-to-body awareness and establishing patterns of well-being mind, body and emotions.

I'd specialized in Network Spinal Analysis (NSA), which helps the nervous system re-organize itself to become more aware of body, mind, and emotion. I had chosen to help people release tension and stress so that they would spontaneously choose quality of life change. I wanted to deliver Chiropractic to help people access innate intelligence and uncover true health. The goal of my wellness facility was to develop new patterns of tension-free living that promoted increased quality of life.

The nervous system is the place where our signals, how we sense the world, and our perceptions are created. In my work, I was trained to understand how a nervous system's integrity can evolve, becoming healthier and stronger. And how we can break old patterns encoded in the nervous system and develop new, stronger ways of living life.

Although my passion was on target, I saw consistent failings and stuck perspectives in women's nervous systems: what was happening?

Mostly women came to me for chiropractic care because they felt that something needed to change, and this often manifested in a physical pain or discomfort. Many times, they were sick and in pain with no allopathic answer. They would arrive at my office feeling misunderstood, misguided and judged. But, when it came to making changes, digging deep, and making life shifts, patients seemed to back off, fall out of care and stop caring.

Digging deep for answers inside the body seemed scary and foreign.

No matter what I said or did there was a very stuck part of our nervous system that rebelled against change (what I now call the Rebel Voices). The push back was so extreme a patient would sometimes just disappear as she was about to awaken into full power.

They wanted the problem fixed but did not want to exit from the boxed-in strategies that had them fixed and rigidly stuck. They would back out of care because someone told them to stop, insurance didn't cover it, or they had money issues. There was a great lack of willingness to understand or communicate, a lack of intuition to educate, a spouse (usually a husband) who said, 'No you can't heal', etc.

Patients did not know they had the power to move beyond stuck situations.

Lack, Lack, Lack...I heard it in one form or another every day.

So, I decided I had to slay this dragon holding women back.

Sometimes their arrival in my office was a search for stress relief, and sometimes it was merely a last resort for those who didn't have any other answers or medication. Many times, it was driven by a sense of desperation, deep-seated pain, and chaos.

Although I faced a lot of resistance there were certain people who would stay despite the resistance. They would naturally start talking to me as I worked on their bodies. And as a Chiropractor, I wanted to help these awakening people. So while I did their bodywork, I'd connect with them, asking about what was happening in their lives. I began to channel spirit and the words would flow out of me.

The messages would come from spirit...
"You deserve more."
"You are amazing."
"You are light."
"I love you."

My spiritually-inspired words became catalysts for amazing life change for my patients. I would help women see greatness in the mirror by speaking it directly to them from spirit.

I intuitively asked them questions that really got them talking, and it was fairly normal that in the first session I'd see tears as clients would open up to relive a trauma or hardship. They'd slowly unwind and process – finding words to tell their story, share emotions, and talk about what was important to them.

And then I found that my channeled, intuitive questions and the answers they elicited were more powerful than the physical work I was doing. I started to create a belief that there was a way to facilitate awareness in people that would allow them to access the changes on their own, at home, work, playing and basically anywhere. I wanted to help create this connection.

I started to create meditations, visualizations and exercises to help women connect inwards.

As I worked on their bodies, all their unprocessed "junk" would pour out of them. No one had ever given them the sacred space to talk about themselves! They would take time with me in authentic conversations having bold explorations of feelings and desires. I immediately saw the connection between the physical work on a body and the stored negativity in a body. The physical work opened up a tank housing deeply-buried trauma, allowing people to pour out their beliefs, thoughts, grief, frustration, etc. After the release, patients would feel better. And they felt inclined to seek more transformation.

This was exciting for both my clients *and* me!

I wanted more, they wanted more, and there was *joy* to healing.

I had discovered through my own healing and awakening to leadership that this was an amazing tool for realizing human potential. This later became my realization of female power.

To serve patients, I had to revamp my business model, providing more than the 15 minutes I'd scheduled initially. I had to leave the chiropractic model of care and shift into a different form of empowered healing. Each client got an hour of work for full processing – low force chiropractic care (that later became energy work), emotional processing of who they were, coaching with intuition and then homework to change life outside of the practice. This last part, highly unusual in a typical Chiropractor's office, was integral, as the clients needed to integrate the information they were learning about themselves and their soul's purpose.

I was becoming a Spiritual Guide more than a Chiropractor.

This channel of mine was not all roses and miracles. We ran into blocks that would stop my clients' progress in making life changes. I saw in women low self-esteem, the inability to see themselves as positive influencers in the world, and a lack of belief that they deserved happiness, health, or prosperity. And, inevitably, many of them would fall out of care.

Intuitively, I knew this was a leadership and empowerment issue – the negativity was winning. It had become so powerful – the trauma, the self-criticism, the doubt, the denial, the excuses, the avoidance – that it was running the show.

I also knew this was an awareness issue: women were not aware of their own leadership power or reason for being here. They needed the life-change strategies, and I knew I had to do something help women dive into these issues and create empowered living.

I had to find an answer to this question: "How do I reach more women with empowerment and transformation?" "How do I keep them on the path to complete transformation?"

My answer from Spirit: "Become a Spiritual Guide."
"You are a Spiritual Messenger."

Over time – and with a lot of writing, clinical study, and guidance from spirit – I realized that the Saboteur inside of the female soul was winning. The self-critical thoughts and restricted beliefs held power over the potential for change. Women had no access to empowerment or their own personal purpose. They needed to start believing that they had the power to be heard, seen, and validated.

It made me crazy knowing that my female clients wanted to deserve more out of life and play big, but they had limited belief systems or tools to help traverse the terrain of self-empowerment and life change. I was very affected by the way women were limited in power, decision making, and self-worth.

I was troubled by the intense amount of work that needed to be done on the planet to help empower women with spirit. And I realized that the clock was ticking and humanity was on a downward slide into controlled healthcare, stifled expression, and limited abundance. I knew in my heart that something had to change and it had to happen fast!

Please remember this was before the age of technology. I was starting with the dinosaurs. No internet, no website, no Facebook, no Twitter, not even Myspace. Yet, I was determined to get the work I was programmed to share out to the world.

I applied my many years of leadership to wellness concepts, energy medicine, coaching women, yoga, meditation and leadership circles. Through it all I decided that I wanted to focus and help women connect to leadership and fully accept our innate ability to Play Big and believe that we deserve more, much more out of life.

I chose women because they made up 95% of my practice. And in embarking on the quest to facilitate Female Leadership, I found that the tools I use for women also work well for men.

I have applied much of what you are reading to many different groups and individuals including corporate teams, direct sales teams, business owners, CEOs, hospitals, spiritual entrepreneurs, new business leaders, parents, couples, healers and doctors.

It is women who come back for more and request the power to change. And in every case the work is the same: first, embrace the feminine form of confident leadership; then, rewire the Saboteur into Play Big mentality and action.

And everything I teach foundationally comes back to tapping into listening to spirit through intuition to change stuck patterns and connect in new and positive ways.

Message From Spirit

There is a wall - in fact, many walls. Layers and layers of protective barriers stop and halt leadership and destiny from happening in a woman's soul. We have been programmed to stop ourselves from feeling, supporting, healing, feeling, or believing. These walls are blocks. The blocks are excuses. And the excuses become bullshit stories of why not to step forward. It's a never ending spiral when a woman cannot face the rebels and stop them.

Your Mind Must Be Opened

"We know that many women have run away thoughts that limit your circumstances. That you do not 'believe' we are here and available to help you find clarity. We are here to show you that you can release the blocks in your mind and you can open to the thoughts of positive spirit. You are worth it."

Love, Spirit

What is the primary wall we have to take down?

Even with the positive physical and emotional care I provided, over HALF of my clients ran up against a wall because the negativity became too much for them to bear. Even when their hearts said, "Heal and change!" their heads and inner voices said, "Stop". The intellectual and analytical brain had been conditioned to stop any feeling that could ultimately provide healing. The mind would rebel against the spiritual messages being sent though me.

Why does this happen? Because people lacked the facilitated education – the foundation – to understand and sustain outside *my office* the practices, improvements, and benefits they were experiencing in *my office*. The home-work was missing. And they depended on me to fix it. And when it all came down to fixing, I could not do it for them.

Message From Spirit

*The FEMALE Mind is a Major Block, an obstacle, and
a barrier to spiritual information. The female channel
has been walled off and wired shut. Most women spend
time wrapped up in run on thoughts that cause huge
distraction. Others use thought to take down confidence.
Constantly blaming, criticizing, and sabotaging.*

They had no idea how to undo their patterns and move beyond the
negativity running their lives. They didn't believe in themselves – they
needed to invest in themselves and their care on their own, and they
didn't know how.

Many women do not know how to move the negative roadblocks out
of our bodies and our emotions; we need the help of our intuition to
accomplish this, but intuition has been limited by our intellect.

Women over think and tend to block intuition.

You see, women in particular are taught to think – and not to feel. For
most women, "Play Big intuition" is not in our programming, nor is it in
our DNA. From a very young age, we are taught to hold back, *not* speak
up, stay quiet, and play small.

Clearly, women are programmed from the inside out to play small.

Why? We were housewives and caretakers for such a long time that we
limited our creative capacity. Feminism only took us so far in our journey,
but it could not break DNA-coded patterns, the generational stress passed
on through family programming. We have become shut off from our own

inner awareness of greatness; for many of us – until we tune into the idea – greatness is only a pipe dream.

It frustrated me as a doctor to see that everything else was winning over female self-value and empowerment. That women didn't want to believe that they held the power and keys to life change. That the sabotage and stuck programming pulled them away from the care that helped them. That ultimately negativity WON.

The Saboteur in their soul was winning.

Self-perception gets damaged by a lack of leadership education at an early age *and* by the contributing factors of trauma. When signals of self-perception and awareness are damaged or hindered, we stop evolving in the world and in society.

It took me 8 years to decode from spirit that this is NOT a health issue, not a weakness issue, not a socioeconomic issue, not an emotional issue, nor a trauma issue.

It is a leadership issue. And the leadership issue is massive.

The issue does not only include women rising up to embrace and own the female form of leadership; it also involves men learning to lead from a different strategy. Men learning to meet women in the middle, on neutral ground, accepting our leadership as valuable.

I call this *leveling the playing field*. Take down the protective barriers and step into collaboration: this is a how *everyone* (women and men) thrive and create together in a place of Play Big.

I am not talking about feminist anger (although some will surface as we break through the walls). I am talking about empowerment: take feminine power back from what no longer serves us and shift this energy to the other side of female intelligence.

I wrote this book to help you understand that there is another side to every story. That we have to look to the contrasting story to get answers to life's struggles. That there are many answers to questions that have been one sided and there is a totally valid way of looking at leadership that does not involve masculine standards of operation. And in this case, Female Leadership can evolve and expand. And anyone can access this new form of leadership at any time.

Women can lead the way: we do this when we venture to the OTHER SIDE of the story.

Why Women?

Women naturally are all of the things I have listed above. And men also have these characteristics when they allow their 'female side' to emerge and exist without fear or judgment – which balances interactions.

That's why I'm here. I want you to understand that accessing Female Leadership is your purpose for being on this earth. It is visionary. It is long-lasting and is the protection of the future. It is your reason for living. It is your impact, your destiny, and your purpose. It is how you express yourself to those around you: your authentic personality.

It is the inside out kind of authenticity and love that our planet needs right now. Desperately needs.

It is heart-centered and kind.

Your leadership can be represented by the choices and decisions you make based on your inner beliefs, not by credentials, title, position, affluence, race, or gender.

Message From Spirit

Pay attention! This message is very important! Leadership in this new form, with a feminine spin, is NOT hierarchy, control, or exclusive power. It's not the guy in the tie or the woman in the suit. It's not mean or manipulative; it's not impersonal or non-emotional. It is not greed.

It's not for the few. It's not for the rich and wealthy and privileged. It's not a carrot-dangling endeavor that you have to work hard to achieve. It's not so far out in your future that you can only hope or scrap for it.

Female Leadership IS accessible to you right now. And this form of leadership is for every body, every gender: it is inclusive. It's humanistic: it's a natural part of who we are to lead each other forward, to inspire each other to move ahead. Leadership is necessary at all socioeconomic and education levels to take action, to contribute to our society, our families, our work places, and our social circles.

The Female Form Of Leadership

"You have a special and unique leadership gift to give. We want you to give this gift as a female leader who embodies change. Embrace the changes you seek as limitless possibilities."

Love, Spirit

So now you know it is important for you to become bigger, Play Bigger, and embrace life. You know that your leadership is key to unlocking the door to success. And as you unlock the doors of change, you can begin to move to the other side of where you are today and access what you want.

We all have a contribution to make to leadership: the biggest contribution is in accepting and honoring that there can be a new way of approaching life, leadership, and living. Once you have bridged this new way of looking at the world, then you can dive into releasing your stuck and sabotaging behaviors in a way that facilitates a new life.

Where we are today as female leaders? And where does the female form of leadership fit into this paradigm shift? Why do women rebel against leadership internally and subconsciously? Why do men rebel against women as leaders and call us bitches and nags (or even worse)? What is the programming that is causing such corrosive behavior?

Why is there such hatred and self-sabotage towards female leadership?

Why do we need changes in leadership? What's the problem? And how can fast forwarding everyone help the stuck problems we all face?

Message From Spirit

The Real Picture

Humans face some serious obstacles in our nervous system programming. Self-awareness is at an all-time LOW and intellectual analytical capacity is at an all-time HIGH. Put simply: we are in our heads way too often. And we have ventured far away from our hearts.

Fear-based living drives our actions. It's everywhere, including our language in media and social media. We are faced everyday with programs and patterns that stop our consciousness upgrades. It is *awareness* and *breaking habitual patterns* that set us free from the prison of our egos.

Men are in control and run the world more than women, with sexism at an all-time high. And the confidence to change fully to resolution with empowerment and without fix-it solutions is still very low, despite all of the alternative healing techniques available for people. Women are put into a box of perfectionism, but when we don't live up to the perfect standards we are a bitch, a slut, or another slur that demeans our mere existence.

The more we venture into a technological world, the further we can move away from self-reflection, inner work, and responsibility for change. This means more need for and reliance on drugs, surgery, fix-it solutions, pain, and hardship. Even social media is a tool that can halt or stop consciousness upgrades from the inside of the soul out.

All of this is the wrong direction for humanity. Why? Because it takes the power and control away from self and puts it in the hands of the few.

We need to change the direction of our focus and shift into expansionary visioning so that humanity can progress.

And in order to make fast changes that will reorganize healthier behaviors, we have to examine how we currently lead. Then we understand where we need to go.

What Has Us Stuck?

Female Leadership has a specific form but it is rejected due to misunderstanding.

So. What is happening in Female Leadership?
What perceptions have us so stuck?

In my trainings and coaching, women report:

- Leadership is repulsive.
- Leadership is aggressive.
- They want nothing to do with leadership.
- They have heard it all before about leadership.
- Leadership is dry and boring.
- Leadership is not for women.

And, women tell me that they believe leaders of all kinds (and at all levels) have become aware that traditional leadership methodologies no longer serve us as humans.

Below, these women define modern-day leadership. Let's call those who embrace the following qualities and styles *as the most important leadership qualities* "The Old Guard. It's a system that is the Patriarchy and has been severely masculinized:

- Headstrong

- Intellectual
- Analytical
- Masculine
- Hierarchical
- Non-feeling
- Non-emotional
- Pain IS gain
- Put your head down and go
- Suit and tie
- Women-at-home model
- Division between masculine and feminine
- Who do I know
- It's a big boy's club
- Domination
- Control
- Feminism acknowledged but woman NOT accepted

When you read their definitions, you can easily see how these descriptions and styles do *not* correspond with modern leadership or modern thinking and ways of life.

Women have not *really* had the chance to rise up and achieve success; we are still being held back and held down in because we live in an "Old Guard" world – and there are two other generations of women to consider, too! We must bridge the gap between gender equality.

The old guard taught women to put up and show up no matter what sacrifices needed to happen. They taught us drive, aggression, and ambition over feeling love and life/work balance.

The newer generations want to have it all: feelings, love, success and family. *Newer* success driven women want to be emotionally present, dynamic, heart centered, community based and intuitive. And these women want money to flow to their businesses.

In order for this to happen fully we need deep change in leadership styles and respect for new forms of leadership, including the feminine form of leadership.

Why Do We Need The Female Form Of Leadership?

I have been guided to choose Female Leadership as the catalyst for creativity and collaboration: it's the foundation of *On the Other Side*. This is not "us against them." Instead, it's an exploration about how we integrate Female Leadership into what we already know.

I want to access the answer to these questions:

- How do we use the female form of leadership to open up, advance, and progress our dreams?

- How can the feminine form of leadership become the way we move beyond restrictions and holding patterns into an amazing life of creative flow and destined purpose?

- How can our intuitive powers become one of the greatest catalysts for world change?

Beyond bridging the gap discussed above, the Female Form of Leadership is necessary to inspire other people to change. When we change, others will be inspired to do so; it's an exponential factor, a domino effect. Women are more comfortable with collaboration, and this, as we will experience in this book, is how we exponentially grow and shift our attitudes.

So, what holds us back from this amazing form of leadership? Why have we become so biased against the patriarchy?

Behind every patriarchal leader, male or female, is unprocessed information: stress, tension, and lack of clarity. This is the land of sabotage and stuck. Most of us use our intellectual brain as a way to avoid and distract ourselves from feeling, connecting, trusting, and being. We have placed distractors and roadblocks in our own way.

Our current model holds the intellectual leader as the most prominent and important form of leader, and sustains a belief that there are only a few leaders among the many people. A position of leadership is earned, credentialed, and determined by status.

This isn't real leadership: it's an illusion, a fake out. It's the wizard behind the curtain who lacks authenticity, heart, emotion, or feeling. It's isolating – it blocks intimacy, halts relationships, decreases productivity, and stunts growth. It lacks a huge part of who we are as humans because it disregards the intuitive, feeling nature of leadership as invaluable and inconsequential.

If we call this *Illusory Leadership*, there can be no lineage to this leadership. What are we to pass to those who come up behind us? There is nothing to hand off: no integrity, substance, or education. It creates inept leadership, false power, false hopes, unrealistic ambitions, expectations and entitlement.

But entitlement to what? What is the vision? Who really has control?

Yes, perhaps this strategy may work for some leaders. Domination, fear, and control have worked for many people, countries, and companies. Its demise is evident and its strategy not foolproof. It is a ticking time bomb waiting to go off at any moment.

Now consider the upcoming leader who is handed the keys by the Old Guard. What happens if there is no heart-centered Female Form of Leadership? One which has taught empowerment, collaboration, and strategies to answer the questions *Who am I? Why am I here? and How can I be true to myself to have the greatest impact on other people's lives?*

When this type of leadership is missing, the operational system of what the Old Guard has put in place will get lost! There is no sustainability because it lacks foundation. All the hard work and connections made will be lost or undone because having the keys to the car doesn't mean you know how to drive it, control it, or take care of it.

Are we saying that Old Guard doesn't pass along knowledge or information? No, not necessarily. We're saying what remains external and fabricated based on someone else's inauthentic self doesn't become internally programmed and encoded.

We need to pass on an intact internal operating system in order for an effective leadership lineage to be passed. That doesn't happen until the upcoming leader has done inquiry work to figure out *Who am I?*, *Why am I here?, and How can I do the best for the good of the most?*

Below are the stories of women who never even knew they had a leader within them. Each was crushed by the type of leadership embodied by the Old Guard, living no purpose beyond what they were currently engaged in. Each was playing small. As each opened up to leadership, she saw herself as an impactful world changer, important influencer, or shift- and mission-driven women. When this happens in women, flow is created – a shifting of tides from the Old Guard to a Play Big perspective.

Leslie: I love this story because it represents a powerful integration of self-recognition, leadership, and purpose. Leslie was dragged by her business partner into a Leadership Energy Clearing Session with me. She was blocked and needed clearing. Honoring her business partner's request, whom she trusted with all her heart, Leslie committed to ONE session. That was all it took. She realized in her clearing of emotional garbage that had been lodged in her body that she belonged in a leadership study. Interestingly, she had no idea *why* for about 3 months!

It hit her suddenly when I gave her permission to see herself as a compassionate leader. Leslie owned predetermined thoughts about leadership that stopped her from seeing herself as a leader. She saw leaders as dry, linear, and analytical - not happy, compassionate, or helpful. I explained to Leslie that her purpose was to lead her business with compassion. And that was the moment that everything changed for both her and her business.

Gwen: Gwen was a powerful business leader of a multi-million-dollar company who already viewed herself as a leader in business but had lost her capability to lead an authentic life, free from stress. Stress had put blinders on her ability to see clearly a path that was peaceful, life-giving, and calm.

Gwen came to me seeking help for her life and relationships. Her job was eating away at her soul and had her stressed to the max. She was unable to see herself as powerful because she was being driven by demands of a super busy life. Gwen realized that she did not need the stress and chaos. And she chose to refocus her energy on her own leadership. Her shift came from leadership study and deciding that moving to an area that supported her growth as a woman in a non-stressful way and engaging more fully as a mother, while running her own company, was the best choice she could make for her mind, body, and emotions. Her purpose was not in stress, nor was it all in money and income: rather, she found herself in balance and love.

Melanie: Melanie came to me for weight loss. She had just left a very toxic marriage and wanted to reclaim her body and health. When she sat down with me, all I could see intuitively was a speaker and coach. I looked at her and said, "You are like me, a speaker and coach."

Melanie was annoyed by my comment because even though she had studied coaching and knew her power as a speaker she had no intention to lead with purpose. Her leadership step was to get out of a marriage and reclaim her health. I honored this request and helped Melanie reach her goal, and 6 years later Melanie, after much self-inquiry and internal review, has made the decision to lead, speak, and coach her own program.

Whether we are leaders in business, leaders of our families, social groups, organizations, institutions, we need self-inquiry. Seeing ourselves as important players in making a contribution happens *not* because someone tells us we are a leader or 'hands us the keys'.

It happens because we have been given or taken an opportunity to become empowered to see our important contribution, to see ourselves as valuable, to ask ourselves the tough questions, and decide on the answers for ourselves!

The Key To Leadership Is Intuition

"You can learn to tune into your heart. Learn to listen to your intuition. And develop a spiritual connection to heal your life and lead from a new place of love."

Love, Spirit

My Story

How did I begin the journey of asking the tough questions?

The keys handed to my by my family were my college education. As long as I went to school and got the best education I could, they told me I could accomplish *anything* I wanted.

Very early on, I realized that leadership was the focal point of my life. I wanted more than just going to school and getting a great job. I wanted to know what my operating manual was for the world. Who is Pam, and what does she have to contribute to the world to help other people? I wanted to discover who I was, what made me important, and what I did best. I wanted my female mission, purpose, and destiny, something that was never taught to me in school or family but was intuitively driven.

Many things in life, including severe depression, caused me to seek powerful forms of spiritual and intuitive healing. This led me to develop into a heart-centered leader. As I developed my heart center, I realized that it was ok to have emotions as a leader. In fact, this is what inspires me to help the world. I also knew that to operate from my heart in this modern world, I needed a strong core, and a healthy body to lead.

I didn't want the keys handed to me from anyone; I wanted to define myself as a female leader based on my purpose and my destiny. It was innate and appeared when I was a teenager.

I wanted more out of life in addition to my good education.

What I discovered is the key to leadership is intuitive and lives in the subconscious of women. And intuition is a very female way of driving business and living life. Why? Because it is quiet and inward. Intuition requires stillness: listening, being present, receiving, psychic sensing, feeling, empowering, growing, sensing, and loving. It is the recognition of soul and the removal of ego and intellect. It requires us to go inwards – and then speak up for who we are and what we believe in, with confidence and truth.

Compare that list to the Old Guard one above, and you'll see a severe contrast between masculine and feminine forms of leadership.

So, let's begin with you. This redefinition of leadership begins with recognizing that maybe somewhere along the path there is something you missed. That there is a deeper meaning to your life that needs your attention.

This begins with the exploring the feminine form of embodying intuition.

Oh, and I know that if you haven't already engaged in this feminine super power that there will be some rebelling. So, hold on for the ride and let me explain why I believe you are intuitive.

My intuitive pathway has shown me that we have tuned out some our greatest resources as women. And this is understandable. In order to keep up with patriarchy, women are taught to be analytical and tuned out from emotional, sensory experiences. Our intuitive powers have been punished, discredited, and dismissed. This happens through statements that I am sure many of you have heard before:

"You're too sensitive!"
"Why are you crying? Stop crying!"
"Stop being so emotional!"
"There is no place for emotion at work."
"I don't have time to talk about that."
"Shut up!"
"Quiet Down."
"SHHHHHHH…."

Message From Spirit

Intuition is the pipeline to feeling our inner calling.
It is the connection to being emotional humans.
It requires us to listen and process.

But for many women in the modern world this is "too time consuming!"

The female form of leadership requires us to get unstuck through intuition, being sensitive, listening, growing from our authentic self. And, when women I consult and speak to turn inward and explore the internal connections and internal factors, they begin to see that the main answer is *intuition*.

I want you to understand that intuition is the connection to your inner knowing or subconscious truth that already KNOWS that you are amazing. Your intuition KNOWS that you have a purpose and destiny. And that you have space to take up in the world.

Intuition is inner knowing that will give you confidence to lead in new ways.

With authentic intuition, the defining questions of leadership are no longer "Who do I know?"; "What do I know?"; "How is it done best?"; "What are your Credentials?".

They become "What is my purpose?"; "Why am I here?"; "How can I be true to myself and have the greatest impact in other people's lives?"

In this process of embracing your leadership, female-style, you will use intuition as a connection to expose and emerge your greatness, destiny, and purpose – with no dividing energy to it. You will break through walls of resistance with intuition; it is the bridge to success.

But it requires you to tune in to what you are feeling and sensing. Starting at the base reality of your life "Where am I TODAY?" "Right Now?"

Message From Spirit

When you know your purpose, why you are here, and how you can be true to yourself, then you will have the greatest impact on other people's lives through business, family, friendships, partnerships, and ultimately through institutions. This is the Female Form of Leadership.

In partaking in this rather new process, you will have push back and resistance, so understanding some of the key concepts to your *On the Other Side* intuition is very important.

Start with these questions:

- Do you see yourself as a leader?
- What do you relate with as a leader?

Know Your Purpose

"There is more meaning to your life that you might have recognized up until this point. We are all at a transition. You have the power to flow with the course of your destiny just by engaging in purpose."

Love, Spirit

Being a successful woman means that you are good with the fact that you might just have a mission, a destiny, or a purpose. Most women have NO idea that they have a purpose and a reason for being here – for becoming a leader. *Get an education/get a job/do a good job/get paid.* OR *Find a spouse/get married/have children/create a family.* These two very solid paths seem to make sense intellectually but lack purpose spiritually.

And, most women view this life as very linear in this way: it's black and white and there is no questioning that there even *may* be a bigger purpose for you.

I'm asking you to see the world in color and understand that your journey is not linear, that there is *most definitely* a bigger purpose for you. That within your job, family, friends, organizations, and institutions that you're currently engaged in, there is a bigger purpose! You can learn to break down the walls and resistance of the material world, intellect, and masculine leadership.

Before you can access the leadership within you, there is a foundational aspect we must explore: your purpose.

How does purpose relate to leadership? Purpose deepens your connection to leadership. It makes leadership meaningful and valuable rather than just a form of control. I've shown you there's a problem: there's a rift and it's time for you to believe that a bridge is important. The rift can be healed by turning from outward focus to inward focus: *Who am I, Why am I here, and What is my purpose?*

Another word for this is destiny, and I believe that all people have a destiny. You don't need to believe that for yourself, but it is certainly something to consider as we begin to explore the leader within you.

Message From Spirit

Destiny

It's a heavy word, so let's break it down.
What is destiny? It's fairly simple, really: your destiny is your reason for being here, the influence you bring to other people, the positive energy you use to affect your life, your family's life, and the life of others. It is also your manifesting power. It is the universe supporting you and working in synchronicity with your inner desires rather than working against you. It is where the world conspires in your favor and things go your way. It is flow and go, rather than struggle and survive.

It's bigger than just getting up and going to work for a paycheck.
It's bigger than just going to school and getting a diploma.
It's bigger than your credentials.

It's looking at yourself from a communal perspective and figuring out
how to live a better life, influencing other people positively, and affecting
communities in positive ways."

Just as negativity can be contagious, so it is with destiny. The energy – the
positive thoughts, actions, beliefs, and ideas – of destiny is also contagious.

This you must buy into before you can fully accept this new form
of leadership.

Here's a concrete example: If as a teacher, I change my perspective on the
kids in my classroom to believe that every child in school *has a reason
to be here*, then I'm going to address them differently, plan my lessons
differently, and approach their education differently. They will not become
mere vessels of the information I impart to them. Instead, we will create a
communal, community-based relationship and focus on working toward
finding the purpose of each. The approach would be honoring the unique
gift(s) in each and every child.

The same is true of leadership: every single one of you has a reason to
be here. That means each of you are not mere vessels of the information
on leadership I impart in this book; instead, *you* will decide, analyze,
consider, and take action based on what you have found is *your purpose,
your destiny*, in leadership.

When you embrace this shift in thinking and share it with others, instead
of delivering it in a hierarchical manner, you'll extend your reach and
bring others along the path with you.

How does this work? If I have confidence, and I give you confidence – two
things happen: First, you pass this along to others, giving them confidence.
Second, if I need strength and you have strength, you will pass that along
to me.

This is mutual respect created by mutual understanding of each other's characteristics of leadership. Any judgment and fear surrounding different styles, needs, and approaches keeps us from a) understanding our purpose, our destiny and b) understanding and respecting each other.

No wonder we can get nothing done.

However, when an understanding of purpose, destiny, strengths, weaknesses, understanding, and respect occur, we are all willing to extend a supportive hand, a reach, to work together. Let's accomplish things! Let's synergize our efforts!

When you find your purpose, you are no longer separate. You come to understand yourself. There is a lack of fear, of self-judgment, control, of "otherness". You are then able to work together without the judgment. You can simply sit as a witness.

"I matter most" changes to "I'm able to witness. I'm able to witness myself. And I'm able to simply witness others, without judgment."

When you can do this, you are more able and willing to change.

Until you know your purpose, you cannot change. You are stuck following someone else's rules and reasons to be here.

If this is enough for you – that's where you are.

If you want to move forward – you want to find out who you are and how that affects other people's lives.

Purpose Exercise:

Where am I today? Look at these words.
Decide what words <u>you</u> use to define <u>your</u> position today.
Then state a polar position of where you want to be.

Today I am *stuck.*
Today I am *overwhelmed.*
Today I am *stressed.*
Today I have a *stone on my chest.*

I **want** to be *free.*
I **want** to *help others.*
I **want** to *breathe.*
I **want** to *connect.*

Notice the 2nd set of words. They're positive. How in the
world would we ever say our purpose is to be *negative, stuck,
overwhelmed, stressed, in crisis?*

Spirit taught me that our purpose speaks to those positive actions,
positive outcomes, and positive behaviors we seek to impart to
the world.

PURPOSE ONLY SPEAKS IN THE POSITIVE!

I know you want to change your behavior immediately! However,
I ask you to sit in this for a little bit and here's why: the stress and
tension you feel may be so strong right now that it will overpower
what you want. It will *keep* you from moving forward.

Sit in it and do what?!

Do the *Purpose With Presence Exercise*: Be aware. Allow and
feel the stress and tension in your life that impedes your purpose
or thwarts your ability to lead. Breathe into it with long deep
breathing to move some of the stress out of your body.

Journaling Exercise:

Get out a journal, notebook or some paper. Free write, allowing yourself, unhindered, to write about where you are today. Choose one of the words to describe where you are *today* and allow your pen to express what you're experiencing as a leader.

Reconnect to what is really happening in your present moment so you can release it and let it go. Once you've written it down, it's outside of you and you can release it from your thoughts. There is now open creative space to move into what you want. Notice how you feel. Do you feel relief? Released?

What is your purpose?

During a divide or times of difficulty, focus your energy back to asking Why am I here? What's my purpose? and How can I make a bigger impact? This grounds your energy, putting it to a more internally-focused, peaceful place.

Release

Through focusing inward, accessing your intuition, and aligning with purpose, you will release some garbage that no longer serves any place in your life.

I want you to override stuck and move in to your calling. I know you're possibly afraid of life change, and you are probably doing *right now* what you do best. I want you to see it's right there already. You just have to see it. To find your purpose, we begin with inquiry, awareness, and intuition. Destiny doesn't fool around; it actually carries you over the obstacles and *through* the shit that has collected in your life.

The shit is only there because you are not riding out your destiny.

There is a masculine program that repeats in our heads and keeps women stuck. This program pushes against all other desires. The only way to achieve your super heightened awareness is to be completely transparent with the stuck components of being female.

We've already discussed that we have no model for Female Leadership and we know this has to be defined. And now it is time to face the obstacles. This is no small task: it will take stamina and follow-through.

In the pages of the next section of this book, I will ask you questions and have you examine concepts that will cleanse your mind of these rebellious patterns. Mind-cleansing is a full flush of the patterning inside of your brain and body and gets you into the heart. As you cleanse your mind and find intuition in your heart you will experience transparency.

Transparency And Allowing Yourself To Be Seen

"We want you to know and acknowledge that as you take down the walls you will begin to reveal your true self. This is called being transparent, open, and honest. Give yourself permission and allow the world to see the real you!"

Love, Spirit

Transparency is the process of revealing your true self in front of people. It's like showing up with your real and raw attitude, sharing what you feel with people instead of hiding your feelings. Transparency does not mean that you have to be rude or disrespectful. It means you express and feel in the presence of others.

I think of transparency as running down the street naked: it's like being nude in front of people.

When most women think about revealing self-expression to people, it rattles them. But, once you start stripping down, revealing your true self, and telling the vulnerability to stop controlling your emotions, you will find a pride and integrity in being real and honest with your feelings and personality.

As you step out in your star power and speak your true self, transparency won't feel as rough.

Message From Spirit

Spirit wants you to know that in order to be transparent, we have to be real. This will help you let go of doing "the right thing", stop seeking approval from friends and family, and remove blocks. As you become transparent in your inner truth, you will step beyond the piles of shit that have kept you hidden and reveal your true leader.

Female Leadership requires that we show up in our feeling self. It is about dealing directly, being real, expressing the truth, and flexing power muscles – no matter how much fear we might feel.

We grant you permission to be real, speak your truth, and open up your honesty.

Female Leadership is about making money, serving a life mission, and being true to our path. In doing this we also have to remember that the female form of leadership is also win-win: loving, open, honest, real, truthful.

It is based on feminine desire and collaboration to fulfill desire.

How do we get there?

In the next chapters about stuck and sabotage I begin to reveal how to achieve real transparency. You'll read about the patterns that hold women back from success in a real and honest way. Look for the real, honest truth about what holds women back. And see there is a soft yet powerful way to navigate through the stuck and sabotage with an intuitive edge.

We have already discussed how women are taught to hold back and play small. This is an innate pattern passed to us by generations of training. But this tide is turning as more and more women show up ask for more, building businesses and launching great ideas.

The *On the Other Side* mind cleanse strategy is designed to help you tune into this greatness and breakthrough patterns through self-awareness of sabotage and stuck.

Transparency begins with examining the "stuck". Before we go any further using the tools of Female Leadership, intuition, and Play Big mentality to become an amazing leader, we must look at the stuck. Stuck is one of those things that just needs to be noticed, and then you can move on.

Being Stuck means you have your blinders on and are just barely motoring through life. You are most likely finding no pleasure in life. If there is any at all, it is in things that don't serve your highest interest. Because women are taught to play small, we have created habits of controlling our lives with unhealthy behaviors that keep us stuck.

I want you to realize that this problem is not going to just vanish without some new overhaul to your operations manual and a new navigation system. You will have to continually practice tuning into the real you to move beyond the stuck. You will want to notice the mind cleanse words and move yourself to the other side of the story.

It is our nervous system patterns and cultural blocks that hold us stuck. It's no small task to overcome, and I say to women all the time in groups, "I need all of you collaborating and uplifting each other because this shit is deep and it is strong. It is so widespread and powerful that we need a huge community of women practicing the same unstuck leadership techniques!"

The good news is it is your intuition and willingness to be transparent in community that will FAST FORWARD you past the stuck and sabotage into your purpose.

My Story

I first began to recognize the magnitude of stuck as a Chiropractor channeling energy and life-force for my clients to open up and flow. What I would see is that our innate intelligence gets turned off or blocked by all the useless information that gets pumped into us along our path. My job was to release the stress and tension of a burdened nervous system to open up life force or the flow of this intelligence – the natural inner knowing – of how to live a healthy, happy, fulfilled life.

Our body informs us of why we're here – we pick it up through sensation or positive feelings. As the nervous system releases and reorganizes tension and patterns, our quality of life changes and improves. A healthy nervous system provides an internal sense of well-being, stronger immune system, ability to manage stress with more Emotional Intelligence (EQ), faster healing power (bounce back). It helps us face life's challenges with ease and empowerment.

But when we have an unhealthy, stressed nervous system, we become the suffering of our circumstances.

In my practice, I saw primarily women and children and began to study their feminine intelligence. I realized there is an enormous deficit because we are not in touch with our spiritual intelligence, our overall health, or our feminine intelligence. We have no idea who we are as women – that we have an important impact in the world.

Most of the women I saw were stuck in some sort of suffering either in pain, relationships failing, lack of money and income, depression, anxiety, chronic fatigue. I wondered, "Why?"

It bothered me deeply why women were so stuck, why these patterns kept showing up, and it also bothered me that it affected their families, which means kids were suffering.

Spirit spoke to me and told me,
"Turn on their power!"
"Teach them to love themselves!"
"Allow the positive energy to flow!"

"Teach them they are intuitive, Pam!"
"They KNOW what to do."

Once women started to turn on their power, they'd bring their kids to me because they realized their kids had been hurt by the women's pain. The women would then suffer more because they'd realize that their own suffering had caused the suffering of other women. So they'd bring me their moms, their friends, their dogs, etc. And this eventually led to them thinking if you can help heal me, you can help heal my business, prosperity and relationships. So they did.

And then they tried to bring me their husbands. They wanted their husbands to be healthy. They wanted their husbands to understand them. But husbands would NOT come down from their tree houses because they thought I was full of shit. In 95% of the cases, women led the way and the men were having none of it. In 5% of the cases, the men brought the woman, and she would have none of it.

The hardest part was watching these women have to ask their husband for the money required to heal themselves, their relationship, or even their children. But the men would absolutely not entertain the idea of investing in this.

Even if they had seen improvement and healing! Even if they knew my work worked!

Many, many women would be so swayed by their husbands and their resistance that they would come back to my office not in their feminine power but back in their masculine paradigm. When they would hit this roadblock it would include a sense of self-righteousness, anger and frustration.

They would spout what the men in their lives were saying: *What she's doing is too spiritual. Too expensive. Too unstudied by the medical field. Unvalidated. Unprecedented. We don't have the money. You can't lead. You are crazy to try. Stop with your pipe dreams.*

Many times this masculine energy was mean, spiteful and demeaning.

Sometimes it felt as if they were spitting on me. Throwing garbage in my lawn. I saw it as rebellious, disrespectful, and closed-minded. And it fed my soul with a desire to make sure women found ways to heal themselves anyway!

This was the patriarchal paradigm pushing back against my business and my way of doing things, which is healing, soft, natural, intuitive, – all very feminine things. I knew in my heart could bring happiness to a stressed-out relationship, family, and household. I was blown away by the resistance and the choice to live in a stressed-out world, full of drama, separation, pain, and suffering.

Many people thought I was crazy. But I was getting results for my clients. Massive results. And there were enough women who were standing up for their needs – taking their power back – and standing up against the patriarchal dissent – to get their needs met and their health back.

That's when I started to move my business from a patriarchal paradigm and created a completely different model. I left insurance, I left Chiropractic, and I decided to create my own empowerment leadership system to awaken health, wellness, and sexual intimacy.

Something outside of me, the universe, started to speak to me loudly directing me to take different actions. I knew I had to define "How can women run successful businesses in a way that includes health?" I knew it had to also include family, balance, healthy and loving relationships, plus financial prosperity. Community empowerment and evolution were very important to this.

In my heart, I knew women had to take power back from lack, pain, suffering, and injustice. They were taught to play small when all they wanted was health and happiness for their family and business.

I asked the Universe for guidance, and I had an inner voice that guided me, taking me deeper and deeper inside my own feminine power source. It was my intuition and connection to the deeper path that allowed me to study, write, teach, and facilitate programs for advancing feminine consciousness.

Some definitions arrived.

Feminine Power: the process of tuning in to inner intuition, which lives in the form of sensation and feeling and the movement of authentic expression. It answers the question, "Who you are as a woman and what is your reason for being here?" Female power explains, "Why am I here? What is my purpose? What is my reason for being?" from a transformational perspective.

Male Power: is dominating, analytical, hierarchical, controlling, manipulative, end-result based, bottom-line based, and competitive. Male power answers the question "How am I providing?" "What am I achieving?" "How have I conquered this quest?" "What is the predictable outcome?"

Why wouldn't the men come? Why was I only seeing women?

How I could teach women to be strong enough to stand up to the domination of the men controlling what they want? Though this was not always the case, loving and supportive relationships and prosperity seemed like only a small percent of my practice.

What I saw in its distilled form was that a woman had an intuition to heal herself, and I would watch that intuition dwindle based on push back from the male counterforce in her life. Her intuition would then be extinguished. She would allow the walls and blocks to become a force field of dissent.

Logically – this doesn't make sense! After seeing Dr. Pam you're healthy, your needs are being met, you go home with energy, and happiness, and everyone around you is getting better. Why don't the husbands see this as wonderful? Everyone is happier! Everyone is better! Why is this a threat?! Why is making big decisions about your life, health, and business so frowned upon?

I created a small circle of women and men who wanted their intuition for healing met. They wanted it with such great fortitude – doing whatever it takes to make that happen – that I knew I must share this leadership with everyone.

And when these clients succeeded in breaking down the barriers, they ultimately did become supported by their spouse and loved ones – in most cases. Most of these clients were women. However, there are men practicing and leading this work throughout the world of transformation.

And so, I knew I needed to face the patriarchy in the face and stare it down.

Introducing female energy into the masculine world is no small task. The patriarchal patterns are real and we have to bust through them. It's a big 'boys club mentality' world.

"Don't bother me with your feminine needs."
"Stay out of my way."
"I don't have time to talk to you."
"Processing is slow and laborious."
"You are crying again?"
"Your life does not matter."
"Stay in the home and do your girly things."
"Just let the men run things."

Silencing.
Interrupting.
Not listening.
Degrading.
Looking down upon.
Name calling.
Labeling.
Sexualizing.
Harassing.
Raping.

This is real. It is crazy. And very painful.

The hard part about all this reality is that woman have adapted to it. We may have feminist viewpoints and *feel like* fighting back, but we have adapted. And we have hidden behind our sabotage, unwilling to change.

In order to change this paradigm, women are going to have to get REAL.

Painfully Real.

What does it mean to be real?

Feeling the real truth in your heart and speaking from that authentic place.

Dealing directly with your truth and inner reality, no matter how difficult, ugly, or uncomfortable it is.

Facing your fears head on.

Getting to the other side of this story.

And staying on the other side of this story.

FACE
THE
STUCK

Adaptability And Comfort Zone

*"You have adapted and become comforted by the discomfort in
your life. But look around you. Look at the swirl of life, the chaos,
and stress. Take a look at how we are really treating each other.
We want this to STOP. And we will show you how."*

Love, Spirit

To access the bigger parts of our lives – the parts that make more money
and experience more love – we have to choose to access this truth inside
and we have to *want* more.

This starting point to overcome what we have become comfortable with in
our lives.

And that requires getting uncomfortable: leave what we "know right now"
and move into a different place that is real and feeling. All of those things
we were told NOT to be? Well. We have to become.

We have to stand up and find communities where we can be heard and
validated in our truth.

We must want women around us who applaud our success, even when they are unsure of their own.

Before delving in to that path, let's take a transparent moment to be really honest with where we are today: examine the depths of our patterns as women.

Message From Spirit

This is where we have to get down and dirty. This is where we separate the truth from the lies. We want you to get this one and understand its value.

The truth is that there is so much more for us to experience. There is no way to move forward as humanity unless we face that truth. But the stuck of denial, avoidance, excuses and blame is so real; we must be honest about the roadblocks to female success that we need to remove.

Why Do We Adapt?

Humans are known for their incredible ability to adapt. In fact, we pride ourselves on overcoming challenges, facing struggles, and a work-hard mentality.

However, some adaptation is negative and harmful. People adapt to being sick, overweight, hypertensive, and judgmental. We also adapt to negative characteristics of leadership: resentment, frustration, fear, greed, denial, etc.

Notice how we have adapted to carrying excess weight.

Notice how we have adapted to suffering and pain, as if it's a natural everyday occurrence.

Notice how we have adapted to toxic relationships and drama.

We have adapted to not smiling or saying hello.

We have adapted to drugs.

We have adapted to kids stealing drugs from our medicine cabinets.

We have adapted to abuse.

We have adapted to drugging ourselves.

We have adapted to being fine.

We have adapted to cancer.

Adaptation asks us to turn another cheek and make up reasons for this being "ok."

This is only a short list of our human adaptations. But are they adaptations at all? Are we really ok?

Restrictions And Limitations

Adaptability is a function of the nervous system. It causes limited awareness to what's really happening in a restricted and limited environment. This is why thought leaders encourage us to leave our cozy Comfort Zones because ultimately, a Comfort Zone doesn't always serve our highest good. Comfort is a liar, making us believe we are secure and safe. It's a false belief that we are ok, when really our lives are at risk.

Staying in our Comfort Zone is how we come to define ourselves in and relate to the world around us through *patterns*. We create these patterns (or rules) for how we're living life based on how we've been raised, what we've learned, and how we're educated. Then these patterns become our reality. We even blame these rules and patterns on previous generations with a sense of pride. We take an attitude that 'this will never change', because 'it's in my family' or 'it's a disease I will never get beyond'.

Patterns give us identity and definition, which loops back around to who we are as leaders. We begin to categorize ourselves as belonging based on title, gender, position, race, etc. This sense of belonging is so powerful it dominates, controls, restricts, and limits.

The Comfort Zone is the space we *adapt* to – the place we get used to, accustomed to – and we start to not only believe the patterns created there, but then we act on them. We tell ourselves, "This is who I am. This is my reality, and this is how I live my life."

Comfort Zones house the feelings that we've adapted to, even if they are negative - like judgment, hatred, resentment, etc. But these feelings become what we know, so it's what we live. It's how discomfort of trauma and abuse can become comfortable. We adapt, we cope, we put up with it, we fake it. We suffer in silence and speak to no one about our pain.

We falsely believe that our pattern is the way life really IS.

It's like a woman who lives with physical abuse from her partner. She adapts to, copes with, and makes excuses for his behavior. She excuses him with, "But I love him" or "He is this way because he drinks too much" or "I can handle getting knocked around".

Suffering in silence, this woman bottles up her pain and shoves it away. Why? Many reasons. But the biggest is she in NOT honoring herself, her leadership, or her power, and this lack translates into pain.

She's become comfortable with how she's defined herself *and* her partner. And one day, she suddenly finds herself stagnant.

This is how it works for all of us. We become comfortable with how we define our self and our world. Then one day, we suddenly find that we are stagnant.

Women choose to stay stuck in some way every day, everywhere.

You'll find it in schools, parenting, businesses, stores, on the street, in the car, and in the media. They choose to stay comfortably uncomfortable. But why?

Limitations Of The Comfort Zone

How can the Comfort Zone feel so comfortable when the emotions we are housing there are so *un*comfortable? Why do we stay there when we feel stuck or harmed with our warped, limited perceptions?

It's simple to understand: The Comfort Zone allows us to see life only with blinders on. In that way, we keep ourselves small, limited, and constricted. We do not see any possibility for change or perspective of what "could be".

For example, perhaps you've told yourself that, "I'm just a manager. I am good at implementing policy and providing structure." This pattern holds you in a Comfort Zone and becomes a power play. It allows you to define yourself, fit in, and put up with what you feel you have no power over.

It makes sense: a woman who wears a title or position then "fits in" is immediately accepted.

A woman who stands out and speaks up is weird, crazy, different, and transparent. The woman who steps out of her Comfort Zone is daring, bold, real, authentic, and powerful. And that is NOT how women are to act or behave!

So many of us choose to stay hidden and "comfortable" even when it threatens our health, sanity, or security. We sacrifice ourselves to the masculine model. Women are scared to be seen and heard as different because it means rocking the boat.

Why is acknowledging this important? When you are trying to access leadership, you *must* redefine and reorganize your thoughts and behavior around a new definition of yourself. This new definition – this new place – *is where you want to begin to leading from.* What is your inner knowing telling you?

Accessing Female Leadership means you must go outside your Comfort Zone to create the new characteristics or self-expressions you're ready to embrace, become, and activate. Those qualities *will* emerge when you use and activate them in your community and create specific action steps that enhance the quality of leadership you've identified.

To get to the other side...you will need to dive in deep and find out who you are inside. It will feel like you're rocking the boat, causing waves, and not fitting in. You'll be breaking through unchartered territory where you will want to redefine to the world that you mean business.

As you realize you don't want to fit in or adapt anymore, you'll have to deal with the push back of the universe. It may seem as if you are on the wrong path because all your past programming to stay stuck will challenge you. Anchor yourself and tether in as a leader.

Rocking The Boat

Susan decided to visit my office for leadership development two times a month. To do this, she had to leave work early, rearrange her family life, and make a place for the new thoughts and beliefs that were appearing in her life.

Ultimately, all of these changes and experiences were very positive and uplifting, but she had to have many conversations with people about her new behaviors and attitudes. She had to reschedule her day to make time for the sessions.

This is a small example of the rearranging you'll do to begin stepping out of the Comfort Zone. When you choose to step out in a new direction, waves of change happen and things need reorganization. New communication and standing up for new behaviors and expectations is required.

This takes energy and desire. The desire to experience something new. The desire to feel better. The desire to trust something different. The desire to make waves of change.

The opposite choice is to stay stuck, limited, sick, lacking, and unhappy.

Stepping Out Of The Comfort Zone

Some amazing potential awaits once you step outside of the Comfort Zone; you'll find amazing characteristics that *you don't even know you have* because they have been masked and kept inaccessible from you.

The return on your investment of time and effort in stepping out is huge: it brings energy, happiness, and true purpose.

I understand how strange this sounds. How hard this is to believe.

But I can't express *how many people* I've seen who have experienced stepping out of their Comfort Zone and found happiness, energy, and themselves on the other side.

Let me share about women who were fearful and stuck. These women desperately needed a push outside of their Comfort Zones to receive new energy and take the blinders off so they could see what they could truly accomplish. Once each did, she created a powerful alternative energy and moved into the Creativity Zone.

Stepping out of the Comfort Zone into clarity is to define who you are as a woman. In my facilitated leadership trainings, I ask women to define leadership and stand up and talk about it. I notice that standing up and defining their strengths and power to a group is a very fearful and uncomfortable place for women. It's like it is wrong or bad to stand up and speak about our positive characteristics. It is wrong to celebrate our self. It is wrong to have power.

I also notice that sharing feelings is very uncomfortable for women in front of a group. We tend to slink back into the chair when asked to share what we really feel. We create many excuses and reasons for our feelings. The minute we *feel*, we back ourselves out of those feelings by trying to explain or validate them.

Women are not familiar with what I call ROAR: **R**adical **O**pportunity **A**ppearing **R**IGHT NOW.

It's a state of getting what you want and deserve from the universe.

We feel uncomfortable with our abundance and achievements. We don't know how to celebrate each other or ourselves in a group. It is very uncomfortable for a woman to celebrate her success or even ask for what she wants in a group.

So how can we change this lack of desire to ROAR – and receive opportunities? Celebrate with other women? Feel accepted and loved for our accomplishments?

Journaling Exercise

What is your ROAR?

Journal about what it would feel like to have a radical opportunity to change your life right now.

What does it mean for you to access your inner ROAR?

Your Creative Zone

*"You all have creative power. It is your birthright to create.
We are always co-creating. We want to help you create more
power in your life to feel inspired with light and love."*

Love, Spirit

The opposite of the Comfort Zone is the Creative Zone, where we see the possibility of what we want and who we ultimately want to be. Here, we get to decide what our goals are and what changes we want to make in our lives! The Creative Zone is where we co-create with spirit to make positive changes.

This is where a Play Big mentality helps us grow and expand. But in my experience, when we are limited and hindered in community, the Creative Zone is impossible to access.

Ultimately we're taking responsibility and ownership. Taking our power back from negativity. We come to believe, "These patterns I've become used to no longer serve me. I am stuck, and I want something more. *And I'm going to create it.*"

Message from Spirit

(I have received this one over and over.)

Women are creators: our creative power lives inside of us. We tap into it by choosing to override denial, stepping into creativity and flow of life purpose. To get there, our creative circuit has to get stronger: we must believe, think, say, and feel, "I want more. I want to achieve more. I want to BE more."

"I allow more light into my life. I lighten my load by releasing burdens and creating love."

Living in the stuck and sabotage makes the Creative Zone feel almost impossible, that the odds are stacked against us. And know that we are all stuck in these self-limiting patterns to some degree.

But we can only do this in community with other people supporting us.

If this doesn't resonate with you right now, try the action steps below and continue to stay with me through the next few chapters as we break down the patterns that hold us stuck. You will come to understand what "taking responsibility and ownership" means to *you*. And then, you'll be able to apply what we've discussed in this chapter.

To engage in creativity, it is important to exercise your birthright.

Action Steps:

How do you create this new circuit to replace and reorganize your limiting Comfort Zone? How do you bridge this gap?

1. Take ownership of improving your life. Identify what you want to become.

Then, you will learn to create intentioned action that removes the sabotaging patterns keeping you stuck. These actions will move you through the *sabotage* (more about sabotage in the next chapter) to your newly-defined, ultimate goal.

Example: "I want to become more authentic." (Here I have clearly identified "what I want to become".)

Goal: "I want to be strong in the face of adversity. I want to stay strong in the face of adversity in my workplace and be real and authentic when facing these challenges."

Comfort Zone Behavior *(i.e. where I am stuck)*: "I am the caretaker to everyone. I mask my own needs and take care of other people instead of facing someone's complaint with authenticity. I don't get my needs met."

Action Steps: "I remain authentic and speak my truth in the moments of difficulty. I am honest. I do not sugar coat anything in the face of adversity, even though it is uncomfortable and difficult."

Likely you've read this example and wondered, "How do I remain authentic? What do I say to speak my truth? What do I do when I meet adversity? What do I say when someone is unhappy with my new role?"

In the following chapters, you will learn more about how to answer those questions. Before you worry too much, try the following exercises to practice this new way of thinking.

2. Define and write about your Comfort Zone by exploring these four questions:

- Where do you feel like you need to make improvements in your life?

- How do you want to be better as a person?

- Is there someone in your life that you look up to, want to emulate, or see as a mentor?

- What qualities and characteristics of that person do you want to possess?

Examples:

I want to be a better parent.

I want to show more love to my husband.

I want to be a better communicator.

I want to stop going to work pissed off at the world.

I want to stop thinking bad thoughts about myself.

3. Explore what you want to create as your ultimate goal.

Examples:

I want to be strong and not sugar coat everything.

I want to not care about being not being liked.

I want to love my job.

I want to wake up happy and energized every morning.

I want to know that my impact on other people's lives matters.

I want to be more present for my children.

I want to build a powerful business.

I want to create multiple streams of revenue for my family and myself.

4. Explore what is standing in your way. What sabotages you?
What tricks you to think you should stay in your Comfort Zone?

Use these prompts for help:

- My excuses include...

- I am in denial of...

- I sit in judgment of...

In the next chapter, we will explore the Saboteur – the Rebel Voices - that want to keep us from reaching our ultimate goal. We will become aware, deconstruct sabotaging behaviors, and move toward the Creative Zone!

Reflection On Female Leadership To Get Out Of The Comfort Zone

Give yourself permission and support: *Permission* is the opposite of all of the above roadblocks. A state of allowing and receiving what we want and desire.

It is a state of allowing ourselves to be present with what we want from life.

Permission is the gateway to the Creative Zone. It begins with *allowing* – when we are open to new ideas and concepts, willing to listen, even when there is push back in our minds.

Allowing creates a space of receptivity where we can build an amazing life. In order to overcome the limitations blocking Female Leadership, we must allow our self some time to reflect. Slow down in life for just a moment. Five minutes in the car. In the shower. In bed at night. Just take a moment to reflect on *allowing* what you truly want and desire to float into life.

Examples:
I allow myself more money.
I give myself permission to heal this marriage.
I am receiving great fortune.
I am allowing my leadership to emerge and I am compassionate.
I allow myself to communicate.
I give myself permission to receive a weekly massage.

Start to use this language in your head, thoughts, and throughout everyday life.

Here's a fact: you cannot do this alone. You will want to surround yourself with women and practices that open you up to receive new information. Allow yourself to be drawn in and capture moments with women who are awake and aware of leadership in a feminine way. You will want to immerse yourself in inner study and open your intuition.

In this process a woman needs permission or validation to get what she really needs from life, and that's where community comes in. It's really important for women to link arms and support each other. Lift each other up.

When we show up in community and ask for what we want and need, other women usually have a solution or support for us. We just have to learn how to move beyond our usual reaction to control or resist.

Give Up Control

"We want you to give it up and give it over to source power.
We want you to turn over your death grip on life and allow more
love to enter your soul. We want you to learn how to love."

Love, Spirit

For the sake of other people in our lives, we've had to put up many false variations of ourselves.

We put on a face that shows that we've got our shit together. This is a form of controlling ourselves to be perceived as having it all together, knowing all the answers, knowing where we're headed, etc. Control puts up a front, a false knowing, under which there is no substance.

In many cases, people put up this facade while their lives are falling apart behind it. Think about drug addiction, failing businesses, fading relationships, pain and suffering, loneliness and isolation, etc.

Control is the Big Liar: it tells us that we can fix anything with medications, surgery, distraction, etc.

Control lacks realness, authenticity, emotional processing, human contact, or connection.

Control shows up in who we surround ourselves with: we choose people who let the mask stay in place and most definitely won't rip it off.

Control is a radical form of adaptability, convincing us that we can buy anything, do anything, go anywhere we want. It convinces us that we've got it all together, and maybe we've even got it better than other people.

Control doesn't fill us in on how unhappy or unfulfilled we are underneath. It has us convinced that the buffering – the Rebel Voices – are enough. It convinces us that Control makes us happy.

We have refused to let our guards down long enough to get still, assess how we're really feeling, and ascertain whether Controls is in our highest interest.

Resistance

A form of control is resistance. We resist doing this spirited work, putting up walls around ourselves, because we don't want to deal with what's inside of us.

The ugliness.
The loneliness.
The negativity.
The shame.

How do we know we're in resistance?

When we know there's something we want. We like. We need. We've heard. Something that inspires us.

And we still don't take action. It's not only that we don't take action... we become kind of a jerk about not taking action.

"That's stuff is totally bullshit".
"That thing is ridiculous."

When we call something "stuff" or a "thing" we know we're in resistance.

When we shut off feelings and walk away, we know we're in resistance.

When we make a story about why we're not engaging, we know we're in resistance.

"I didn't want to be on that team anyway."
"I didn't want to be in a relationship anyway."

Resistance is a tension in the body. It's a feeling of building up tension – and we can move away from it and ignore it. Or we can move into the tension and feel it, engage in it, express it, and get stronger from it. This will move into the other side of victory – whatever that is for each of us.

Most people don't know how to do this. They ignore the tension, shove it away, and call it names.

That is resistance.

We deal with resistance by feeling the tension, living with it and allowing it to build in the system. If it moves through us, it becomes a vital life force to create the things we want.

It just doesn't feel good.

And that's OK because moving through the resistance put ideas into motion, creating energy and opportunity.

Steve Jobs just didn't create Apple out of ease. He had to move through so much resistance, including getting fired from his own company. To achieve his empire, he had to move through difficult feelings, tension, resistance.

Imagine our world without Apple. Or technology. Or even electricity. The only reason we have these things in our world is because people have been willing to move through resistance to get to the other side.

Are you willing to shake in your shoes? To be transparent? To speak up for yourself when you really don't want to say anything?

Are you ready to win the war on resistance? Are you ready to squash your Rebel Voices?

Identify Your Rebel Voices

When we start to grant ourselves permission to open, allow, and receive, our Comfort Zone will rebel. The patterns we've created have very powerful inner voices associated with them. I call the voices that push back at our plan to receive what we desire the Rebel Voices.

Exercise

Release the Rebels

All of a sudden you step out of your comfort zone and the judgey voices begin. These are the Rebel Voices: once we realize they're there, we start to notice how ugly and toxic they are.

Be prepared to work through them without judging them or yourself – because it's not a pretty process if you get hard on yourself.

The way to neutralize the Rebel Voices is to merely accept that your brain is trying to protect you. It's trying to keep you safe – it doesn't want you to take chances.

Your brain knows what it knows, and until you decide to build stronger, more positive patterns of thought and behavior that will *create where you want to go in your life, those Rebel Voices will keep you stuck.*

Exercise (cont'd)

1. First, hear the Rebel Voices. Describe what they are saying:
   - *I can't do that because it's stupid.*
   - *If you stand on that stage and speak you'll make a fool out of yourself.*
   - *What if you say the wrong thing?*
   - *What if you do the wrong thing?*
   - *You can't do that because you don't have the credentials.*
   - *Who do you think you are?*

   Then, name these voices:
   Cynical. Negative. Toxic. Judgmental. Etc.

   Now, you can recognize them based on their negative qualities. See those voices for what they are and name them. Identifying them takes away their power.

2. Express the voices: How can you let them express themselves until they're exhausted? Ask your Rebel Voice ALL the reasons why you shouldn't step forward in your life. Write them down and let it flow *without judgment*.

3. Re-create the Rebel into what you want. On the other side of the Rebel is the **truth** of who you are as a human being. Now, *allow* the other part of you – the one that wants what you want, the one that is motivated. Go through the same process: Hear the Truth Voices. Identify them. Let them speak. What do you want to become?

4. Take action: Examine the aspects that only serve you and move you toward your goal. How do you move forward?

Book that speaking gig – even though you're afraid of saying the wrong thing on stage.

Exercise (cont'd)

Write that book – even though you have a fear of grammar, you know you have an author inside.

The most vital advice I can give: **hire an expert** to help guide you through this process! The Rebel **will** tell you not to hire an expert. But *know* that you need someone to guide and support you – it's WORTH the time *and* investment to get you to your goal!

Stop Judgment

"Allow your life to be loving, supportive and caring."

Love, Spirit

Why do people judge?

Why do we judge?

Well, judgment is a protection, something we use to block the rest of the world from coming in. When we judge something, we distance it from ourselves.

But, this also blocks our possibilities and opportunities.

If I deem a person 'too self-absorbed' to work with me, how do I know I didn't just push away someone amazing?

The list of judgments and projections of ideas and ideology on to people and groups of people goes on and on. But in a nutshell, judgment limits, restricts, and constricts. It also keeps us safe and sound.

Judgment pushes away what the world can offer us. The world says, "I want you to meet this person!" but our brain says, "Ohhhhh no. This person is X, Y, and Z", putting labels on people to keep them at arm's length. Categorizing them creates a separation and a distance from us, which stops relationships from happening, growing, or existing.

Judgment is embedded in us. Many of us are married to our judgment. It becomes a self-defining mechanism that separates us from others.

For example, if I define a person as "X" and categorize the person as "X", (or other – different from me) then I am free to categorize myself as I see fit – different from Person X and ok with exactly who I am. It somehow allows my definition of self to be acceptable.

But here's the thing: your definition of yourself is acceptable whether you judge that other person or not. Who you are is perfectly acceptable right now!

Judgment is built on self-righteousness. It gives us a sense of our own value: how we define ourselves and create boundaries.

But, it's a double-edged sword, and here's why: it allows us to cast out the self-righteousness toward someone else, AND THEN it then easily turns back on ourselves.

In other words, we become our own worst enemy!

How? Because our judgment comes back to hurt us in the form of a very strong Inner Critic. The judgmental thoughts and words we hurl so easily at others quickly come back and hurt us.

And when we live from this place, we attract drama – life becomes one big distraction.

When judgment is our default, the world becomes a bad place. How so?

Well, when we only think about others' negative qualities, we believe that's what they can only see in us. We start to believe that the only solution for "negative" or "bad" is more negative and bad.

And from this place, love, healing, intuition are not viable solutions because of where our brains and our subconscious are.

When you're in a place of judgment, even goodness becomes a place of negativity, becomes your enemy. When love is put in front of people who are so strongly committed to their judgment, they can't see it, believe it, or even stand it.

I see this in the business world all the time. The distractions, judgments, and critical thoughts, create a giant drama pit, stunting business success and growth.

If you're saying to yourself at this point, "Holy crap! This is me!" that's ok! This is not a place to bring in self-criticism and self-blame.

If you're saying "This is me!" this is your point of change. This is where you decide that things can be different. That things will be different.

It's important to understand that your judgment comes from fear. In order to heal it, we have to look at fear.

We are afraid of our own greatness, our own positivity, our own amazingness. If you've identified yourself as judgmental, as you're reading these words, you're thinking, "Come ON. I'm not great. I'm not positive. I'm not amazing."

Yes, this is tough work. The way to move beyond the judgment is to separate the qualities and move them into compartments.

Polarity Exercise:

On a piece of paper, write "Judgmental and Negative" as a category at the top. In a brain dump, write a list of all the negative, critical thoughts you have about <u>yourself</u>. Add in the qualities you think about <u>others</u> *after you're done with yourself.* When you look at it, know you're not taking ownership: you're dumping it to get out of yourself and your head. Leave it there.

Now create a "Positive" category: list all the *possible* and *potential* positive qualities about yourself. You may have a hard time with this because you have a strong Inner Critic. Really think about positive qualities and characteristics that someone else has said to you, even once, even in passing. Dump all the potential positive characteristics from your brain.

Now, pick **one** of the positive qualities you feel is most possible to believe as true. Your subconscious brain will show you that this is the one because you can feel it inside your body as a vibration. Write this word down, turn it into a Guiding Mantra that your brain can believe, using positive language.

For example, instead of "I'm not a failure", write "I am successful."

Instead of "I'm not smart enough", write "I am totally capable."

Instead of "I'm so weak", write "I am strong and full of energy."

You must practice this mantra all the time: see it, say it, think it, feel it. Bring it with you daily. Put it on your mirror. Write it down all the time. Put it as a reminder on your phone.

When the negative creeps back in (which it will), the word you need to strongly say is, "STOP." Then you return to your Guiding Mantra.

Getting rid of judgment is a practice, not a 'perfect'. Once you start to get a taste of living life outside of judgment's harsh winter, suddenly the climate changes and feels welcoming, warm, inviting.

You won't ever want to go back to the harsh place.

That's why your statement – your Guiding Mantra – is so vital.
This statement becomes your path to finding your value, your purpose.

Judgment is the gatekeeper, and once you pass through it, you enter into the true purpose of *your* life's work, *your* reason for being here.

The fastest path through judgment is your subconscious: once you break this pattern, the light is shed on a new way of thinking – an awakening of sorts. And you will want to follow that light, even when negative, judgmental, dark thoughts come in.

The Saboteur

"You are stuck because you keep sabotaging yourself. We want you to move beyond these self-limiting behaviors and patterns to experience more joy in your life."

Love, Spirit

Rebel Voices are deeply rooted in sabotage. The sabotage is there to "protect you." (Or at least it thinks it is!)

The Saboteur is the part of ourselves keeping us in a Comfort Zone, not always serving our highest and best interest. These thoughts, feeling, beliefs, opinions, and behaviors stand in the way of our progress, productivity, and happiness.

Sabotage keeps us stuck in habitual behaviors, especially the ones that don't necessarily serve our purpose for why we're here. In many cases, Rebel Voices create stories and thoughts in our head that keep us so far away from accessing the truth that it *becomes* the truth – it becomes reality!

Here's what you need to remember: your dream is so *unrealistic* to your Saboteur! You'll hear voices say, "You can't do this. You're not good enough. You'll never make it. You don't deserve that. You'll fail if you try."

Ultimately, our Rebel Voices are our dream busters – they destroy the things we want to accomplish in life. Rebel Voices break our dreams into shards and keep us stuck.

When we buy into what the Rebel Voices are promoting – the Saboteur – we wonder why we'd even bother to go for the dream? It will just seem too hard, too unreachable, too far away. Most people, at this point, rationalize themselves out of their dream in order to stay with the Saboteur. They choose sabotaging over dreaming.

Why We Choose Sabotage

Usually sabotage is built on a foundation of survival from past programming. When something traumatic has happened in our life, our nervous system creates an imprint, a habitual behavior, attitude, and/or posture toward life. This blocks change.

These traumas can be micro-traumas of repetitive behavior onto a child: *Don't do that! You'll never make it. Stop crying – don't feel your feelings. Boys will be boys. You're fat. You're selfish.*

These are statements that our parents, siblings, teachers, or important people in our lives teach us from the outside in. It's a storyline that we continue to live. But why?

Because neurological circuits have been created through past programming of how we were raised, our traumas, and what we were taught. And these imprint habits. These habits build the patterns.

Here's how sabotage works...
Past Trauma > Imprint to Nervous System > Sabotaging Behaviors Emerge > Repeat

Many times, the Saboteur is an influencer or figure of authority telling us who we are and how we should be. This has defined our reality for us rather than giving us the tools to find out who we are on our own.

This is why society lacks leadership! Many of us were not raised to know who we are authentically. And because we haven't gotten the chance to define ourselves, we don't know how to lead our lives from the authentic goodness from our soul. Sabotage keeps us so far away from ourselves that we don't even know ourselves.

Message From Spirit

Squelch the Saboteur
The way to shift is to uncover who we are from the inside out: it's what we call Authenticity.

Authenticity comes from the word "origin". It means 'to be original'. When we teach Authenticity, we ask the Saboteur to step aside or resolve itself so the authentic self can appear or emerge. Of course, this means we have to remove the inauthentic blocks on our true identity.

Authenticity vs. Sabotage

You will come to recognize Authenticity by way of your higher thoughts and feelings. Authenticity, which is your life purpose, *only speaks to you in the positive*. It's going to say, "Yes, you can go this way, and here's how you do it."

It will validate you. Strengthen you. Give you courage, bravery, and confidence.

Authenticity will also speak to you through feelings: joy, love, gratitude, and happiness. These feelings are accompanied by a sense of fulfillment.

Walking your authentic path IS challenging. In doing this work, you will learn to identify which is a *challenge of purpose vs. which is a Saboteur holding you back.*

Expect to develop a sense of a heightened awareness. The work won't be easy or always feel good, but it WILL provide you with a sense of calm. Conversely, recognize that the Saboteur *likes* you to struggle, feel a sense of lack, and have to fight, blame, and deny yourself the positives of Authenticity.

Sabotage will speak to you in terms of feeling resentment, anger, frustration, overwhelm, confusion, fear, and pain.

Walking your Saboteur path is a different kind of challenge. Sabotage is accompanied by a sense of skimming the surface of your life – you will constantly feel anxiety, doubt, and fear. There is often a sense of being lost or not really knowing, so instead you just do what other people tell you.

Overcome Sabotage

Usually when we get to this point, we often think life is a mess and that it's chaotic all the time. We must stop and find out where we're stuck so we can move forward, overcome Sabotage, and become a Leader.

To get Sabotage out of the way, we must ask and explore the answers to some difficult questions.

Exercise:

Start here if you're ready to move your Saboteur.

1. What is the thing that keeps you stuck? You'll know you're stuck because this thing...

    - Sucks life out of you.

    - Keeps you moving so fast that you don't have time to reflect.

    - Causes feelings of self-loathing.

    - Causes feelings of self-doubt.

    - Causes feelings of suffering – nothing seems to work.

    - Causes you to feel like a victim – you have no control over your life.

    - Numbs you. You feel withdrawn and sunken in.

    - Has adapted you to things that are not okay.

    - Makes you feel like you don't want to take up space in the world.

2. After you identify the thing that keeps you stuck, explore *what do you do about it?*

    - Acknowledge that you're stuck. Write it down. Say it out loud. Think about it by addressing it.

    - Find out the details of how you're giving your power away to the Saboteur. What parts of yourself are you giving away to negativity? Where – or to whom – are you giving away your power?

Acknowledge that this is difficult work! And once you've identified what's got you stuck, you can move forward.

From Saboteur To Leader

The following questions will move you forward through the blocks that the Saboteur has created and the feelings that want to push you back into your past programming.

Trust that your Inner Leader knows how to get you unstuck and lead you forward. This requires authentic action on your part!

Journaling Exercise:

Answer each question honestly and thoroughly to activate your Inner Leader:

1. **What is leadership to you?**
   What descriptors would <u>you</u> use to describe the leadership you've seen in your life and those who you look up to as leaders?

2. **What characteristics and traits would <u>your</u> Inner Leader use to get to your life's purpose?**
   These might be different than the ones you identified above.

3. **How are you a leader?**
   This is a difficult question because most people don't see themselves as leaders. Tap inside of <u>you</u> to see yourself as a leader. By developing creative leadership qualities inside of yourself, you'll give yourself the momentum to move out of wherever you are stuck.

Examples of women who did the work – and found where they are leaders:

- Mary's husband is very unhappy at work and his attitude and energy negatively affect the whole family's dynamic. Mary realized that if *she* could strengthen her own leadership and her own happiness, that she could lead her husband forward to create life changes that could lead to his happiness.

- Jennifer never saw herself as a leader but was asked to participate in a leadership workshop at work. Out of duty, she showed up but was resistant, quiet, and resentful during the session. However, when asked the questions above, she began to reframe how she saw herself as a participant in her community. She decided that this inner self-work was important to her *and* those she works with. She became deeply affected by being able to herself as a leader in different ways, including her role at work and in her family. One shift she made was that she decided someone can be an *authentic leader* – true to who one really is and not putting on a mask to play the role.

- Sue came into leadership training believing that she didn't need it. She never saw herself as a leader and was happy to "just do my job." She says, "I came here believing there is only one form of leader – hierarchical, controlling, and with credentials. And I found out there are more characteristics to leaders than I ever thought possible."

She came up with an incredible list of descriptors:

Compassionate	*Approachable*	*Truthful*
Brave	*Available*	*Collaborative*
Proactive	*Aware*	*Present*
Inclusive	*Inspiring*	*Loving*
Dialoging	*Creative*	

Journaling Exercise:

What is authentic leadership to you?

Knowing you can create your leadership into anything you want it to be – to get you unstuck – what leadership qualities can you write down to lead you out of the "stuck" space?

Conquer The Rebel

*"There is a rebellion inside of you that keeps you stuck.
The rebel voice keeps you in avoidance, denial, and excuses.
We want you to move beyond the rebel and take
proactive action to change your life!"*

Love, Spirit

There is a voice that has been programmed into us that doesn't want things to change. Even though we might be happier, energetic, positive, The Rebel ultimately scares people. But when it's conquered, it's incredibly powerful.

Jen's Story

I'm an accountability coach who helps people get the goals they say they've set but have yet to achieve. My husband asked me to meet with a colleague of his, a wealthy older man who wanted to write a book.

When I met him, he spent over an hour talking about himself in grandiose terms. I took notes, trying to get a sense of who he was, but 30 minutes in I realized I'd never be able to coach him. He spoke openly of "needing someone to manage me".

Nope. That is not what I do now.

In the old days, my Rebel Voices would've won. I would have figured out <u>how</u> to make it work. <u>How</u> to help him. <u>How</u> to "manage" him. Why? Because I would've been flattered that he wanted to hire me. Me! I mean, who am I? What am I worth?

My Rebel Voices would've said, "Yes, it will be a lot of work, but you'll make money! And he's <u>choosing</u> you! This might be your only chance!" My ego would've been running the show.

But the Rebel Voices did not win today. Not now.

I repeatedly tried to redirect him, asking him my usual coaching-style questions. He rebuffed and skirted around them, and then I put an end to the conversation. It was far easier than I thought.

I said, "It seems like you're looking for someone else to do the heavy lifting. Is that true?"

And he was a bit surprised, like he wasn't used to having anyone – much less a younger woman – call him out and be direct.

And he said, "Yep. That's about it."

He'd just made it really easy for me. "Ah. I understand. But that's not what I do. I guess I'm not a good fit to help you with your project."

I couldn't believe it! I didn't apologize. I didn't give him a million reasons or excuses. I squelched the Rebel Voices and simply said, "No". It felt incredible.

I knew at that moment that I'd become a different person. I'd grown in a way I hadn't even expected. I conquered my Rebel Voices with zest. I cannot express how good it felt, and no one died, rejected me, or was even sad. It was fantastic. (It's kind of addictive, too).

Jen's story is not the norm. Why not? Because there is a huge fear of the reorganization of change from both women and men.

Can we manage the shifts that occur as the old falls off and the new comes in? When we worry, "Is it manageable?", this becomes our fear, and thus, we stay stuck.

We are used to the masculine powers controlling our powers to transform, and when we challenge it with a feminine model, we aren't sure what's on the other side.

Here's another challenge: the feminine model is slower. No one is telling us, "Here's how you access the feminine model for *money making*." We may understand the feminine model for *transformation*, but not for feminine leadership and feminine financial prosperity.

That is my goal: I want to create a model for feminine leadership and financial prosperity. We can have all our transformation done, but if we don't use it with leadership and making money, we are not going to be on the same realm as the masculine model.

To rise up and feel strong in our power is feeling powerful enough to...

- Stand in my truth in a business meeting with a man who is typically patriarchal.
- Stand in my truth when talking about my journey with inner feminine power and someone doesn't get it.
- Find the resources to do a program I want to when my husband won't pay for my inner healing.
- Say yes to my own intuitions and act on them, even though my Rebel Voices might be saying, "No! Stop!".

How do we do this?

Well, ego creates hierarchy, controlling its environment, manipulating or rationalizing data, and bullying us. Remaining separate and in control, the ego keeps life mechanical and material-based – with no sense of discovery of oneness, life purpose, or spirit.

It is ego that creates Rebel Voices in the head that limit, restrict, and constrict our ability to grow as leaders and as human beings.

If you want access to growth, you must first understand that your ego will *always* work against that. Your ego paints the picture that you already have everything you need, materially. It's protecting you in that way, really.

Second, you must learn how to neutralize the ego. This takes some work and requires you to create "Neutral Ground", helping you balance the ego and the deeper connection to yourself. Without establishing Neutral Ground, the ego splices off your deeper connection to humanity.

Message From Spirit

The Disruptive Ego

To tap into our inner source of greatness, we need
to create space - because our ego will rear it

Remember that the ego is the disrupter to
growth, change, discomfort, or pain. It will tell
us to go back to the comfort zone – i.e. what we
know to be true (the hierarchy, the system, etc.) –
because its job is to protect us from harm.
It keeps us separate from community, from
oneness, from believing there is something greater
in the universe to be experienced and enjoyed.
Shead. The ego, inevitably, resists, pushes back
against change, and keeps us stuck.

Neutral Ground

What is Neutral Ground?
It's an energy we hold in our body that allows change to happen without our becoming inflamed, emotionally disrupted, or abandoned. Neutral Ground creates a space for spiritual connection, intimacy, etc., which the ego will push out of the way.

It's important because some of the things we uncover as we dive into our purpose and reason for being here are *really* uncomfortable.

What we find out about ourselves as leaders as we grow and become connected can disrupt what we know to be true about our life currently.

In other words, the ego will fight back, and that's why we set this Neutral Ground stage.

How do you get to Neutral Ground?
We need to achieve a sense of relaxed openness to allow us to receive information from the higher self – the universal consciousness. This provides a greater sense of knowing that we are all one in this world and are in this together.

This kind of thinking is the opposite of what the ego does. Neutral Ground creates a space to look at ourselves in relation to our title, credentials, and position. Our egoism. When we can see that – when we become aware of those titles, credentials, and positions – we see how we've picked up ways to we define ourselves by these external definitions.

The Mind Cleanse is a way to create Neutral Ground through awareness and allows us to look at ourselves without judgment. When judgment is gone, we decide which changes we want to make to grow as a leader and as a human being.

Exercise:

Let's practice!

- Prepare a mental space to recognize and become aware of the Rebel Voices of the ego and erase them from the mind. Find a quiet seat and get comfortable.

- Begin with awareness. What thoughts are going on inside your head? Notice them. Acknowledge them.

- Choose a word, symbol, or phrase that captures those thoughts. Most of our thoughts fall into the categories of control, resistance, limitation, constriction, and restriction. The ego is going to try to limit our ability to open up purpose beyond these categories, where our minds are comfortable.

- Close your eyes and imagine there is a blackboard/ whiteboard in front of you. Mentally write your word, symbol, or phrase on the blackboard – see it, then acknowledge it by saying "Yes" out loud.

- Then, breathe deeply into this word, symbol, or phrase and begin to mentally erase it from the board. Keep your eyes closed, and keep breathing deeply until it is completely gone. You may imagine, as you breathe in and out, that you are blowing the chalk off the chalkboard.

- When it's gone, keep breathing and replace that word with a new one: a positive word, symbol, or phrase that defines you or what you want to become. Examples: *open, trusting, compassionate, loving, joyful, worthy, peaceful, flexible, calm, creative...*

- When that new word, symbol, or phrase is mentally written on the chalkboard, keep breathing and allow this word to fill your brain.

Exercise (cont'd):

- Taking it to the next level: Imagine yourself as this person defined or identified in this new word, symbol, or phrase. See or feel yourself as this person. Experience yourself in this new form. Feel this energy fill your heart center. You may feel a reaction: your face may relax, stress may release from your body, and breathing may become easier, tingling may occur in your extremities. You may feel lighter, freer, and happier. You may feel a return to "yourself" that you haven't experienced in a long time.

- It is from this state of ease and relaxation that you ask yourself, "There is something more that I need to do with my life. What is it?" This state is where you can get information about your purpose.

I must be honest with you here. This is the place where most people run – it is where the ego takes over, saying, "NOPE. I'm not doing this work."

Your Feelings

All of the information that hasn't been dealt with – all of the life issues and challenges that have never been processed – may surface, and that will bring up *feelings*. These feelings can be overwhelming.

I have had people disappear after committing to this work; they really get the program, they really want changes, and then it gets really uncomfortable.

They blame their problems on something other than what is really causing their problems, and they run. My goal is to provide tools to you to help you move *through* (and not away from) this very uncomfortable time.

You have to be willing to actively participate, practice and work your own program if you want to see change. It has to become part of your lifestyle – it's not a quick fix, because that's not sustainable.

This is why The Witness is so important for creating neutrality as you begin to open up your purpose. In this final part of the chapter, we will understand how to use The Witness to both provide Neutral Ground and coach yourself through the tough times.

The Witness

When you're able to step out in front of yourself and witness yourself, you gain the ability to coach yourself. The Witness is an inner coach who only is not only aware, but can also implement action in a productive way that gets results.

For example: if you constantly feel angry, your review of the Saboteur may show that you no longer want to feel and behave with anger – instead you want peace. The Witness comes into play as an inner coach that you activate.

How? You decide you no longer want to *indulge* any angry undesirable behaviors or thoughts. Instead you want to use your replacement word – the positive word from your Mind Cleanse.

The Witness activates, asking you, "Which behavior is life-giving?" or "Which thought is life-draining?" The Witness allows you to move beyond awareness and *into action*. You begin to ask yourself, "How can I find peace? How can I re-organize my life to find peace?"

The Witness knows what's better for your spirit – it moves you beyond your ego. However, it's the hardest place to be and creates discomfort because it requires dedication to a path you may not be used to.

When we've achieved Neutral Ground, we have created a place to connect to our spiritual observer and see clearly and realistically how we cast judgments upon others and ourselves. Our Female Leadership process allows us to be 110% real and honest with ourselves, positive or negative, without judgment. It's where the mask comes off and we can begin to take responsibility for our negative thoughts and Rebel Voices.

We come back to our breath – and our Witness allows us to, in this safe place, take responsibility for our actions in the world and begin to make the changes we want to make.

The conversion from what is draining you to what can give you energy, power, and life is *challenging*.

AND it will ultimately change your leadership!

In our next chapter, we learn how to not disappear during this time and how to take responsibility for change.

MOVE INTO YOUR POWER

Build Inner Strength

"You will need strength, willpower, and the desire to move on from the Rebel. We want to strengthen you with positive voices, thoughts, and feelings. You deserve motivation and transformation."

Love, Spirit

Standing up to the Rebel Voices takes a lot of what I like to call Inner Strength. It is the, "I am moving forward towards my dream no matter what!" feeling.

Have you ever felt something pushing back at you? Like, you know you're ready to take a step forwards, but the asshole of the universe pushes back at you?

Sometimes the universe will throw up a sign that we're on the wrong path.

It could be the thought, "I'm a fraud". The scripts start spinning, and the self-doubt creeps in.

Sometimes it's external (in)validation from a source outside of us – that holds some power over us – that says, "You're stupid for trying. You're not good enough."

I've experienced this personally. Sometimes I feel like my face is being shoved in the mud, like I'm a small child being told I'm not good enough. My internal voices tell me I'm doing the wrong thing or I am never going to make it or how dare I even try!

I can relate to people who never step out on their path or seek their purpose because the challenges that come up really require Inner Strength.

And unfortunately, there is no other way to move through it other than to strengthen inner knowing.

From the bottom of our being, from the base of who we are, strength has to come *through* us. It's the posture of success: an energy that holds us erect, not schlumping along in the face of adversity or giving up.

Inner Strength shows us that we know how to pick ourselves up, move forward, accomplish the task, and take action, *despite* the push back.

Inner Strength is feeling the push back from the universe (or from our self or someone else) and saying, "Watch me do it anyway."

Sometimes we believe that a higher intelligence (a voice from inside or from someone else) is squashing our intuition, our behavior, our capabilities. Inner Strength is rising up against that, even when our self-doubt says, "You can't". Inner Strength says, "I'm going to *anyway*. I know that this is the right path for me."

There are 3 fast-forward buttons to implement to strengthen and engage Inner Strength.

1. Begin to lead from your purpose with action:

   - **Accept** that you need to take a productive leadership role. Own your leadership.

   - **Know** that you have a purpose as a leader and begin to speak about it.

- **Discover** your purpose – if you don't already know it.
- **Stay focused**: ignore the Rebel Voices, the Saboteur, and the naysayers.
- **Practice** the relevant tools that you need to step out in your power.
  - If you want to become a speaker, then practice becoming a speaker.
  - If you want to teach yoga, then practice yoga.
  - If you want to leave your job, you practice on someone safe, preparing to take action.
  - Get comfortable and prepare so you can feel strong enough to do it.
  - Ask yourself, "What pieces of my picture do I need to practice to get where I need to go in my life?"
- **Participate** in a deeper level with yourself. Journal/reflect/get to know yourself. See yourself in a positive way, and heal where you need to heal.
  - Integrate this practice into your life. Make space for it.
  - Move the world and make space for your goal to happen.
- **Create** your own program
  (leaving a job, strengthening relationships, etc.)

2. Follow and implement your strategy using tools:
   - This is more the masculine side of this work: make sure you **activate** and **implement** what you really want to achieve.
   - Set deadlines, create goals, make and follow through on decisions. Create necessary programming and tools, stay on the path despite the pushes from the universe to sideline or distract you.
   - Know that if doing XYZ produces your end result, you've got to be willing to push through to get to that end result. Most people will stop before completion. This is why **community** is vital.

3. Connect with a supportive community.
   - Find a support structure that makes sure you activate – that supports you in the action steps you're taking in a positive and productive way. This might be a support group, a mastermind, or a coach.

- It could be as simple as a buddy system: a group of friends with a similar goal/interest, a women's circle for deeper introspective work and healing, or a networking group of some sort (a mom's network, a Facebook group, a professional group, etc.)

- The community must have the intention to support the goals you're trying to achieve. You need to feel heard, be able to share freely. If you keep the challenges to yourself, you will be tempted to not take action. So, talk about it in a safe place, and get real affirmative about it. In other words, stop asking questions and turn what you want into a statement. *I'm going to write a book* instead of *Should I write a book?* has a very different outcome.

The world will give you so many reasons to stay stuck and not achieve your purpose. The universe can keep you fatigued, which you may take as a sign to not move forward, keeping you paralyzed.

Find a place, a community, where you can release that, process your purpose, excise your excuses, and allow you to re-create your belief (again, over and over) that you can do this! Believe that action is not only possible but necessary.

Exercise:

Journal on these questions.

How? Through a process of acceptance.

- Do you accept that you are valuable?

- Do you accept that you are worthy of living your purpose?

- Do you accept that you need a community that wants you to thrive and grow?

Until you accept those things, you will stay stuck. And if you don't, you need to give yourself permission.

Female Training

We are trained to look to the external world, certifications, degrees, etc. for validation that we can live our purpose. All we need is our inner strength. We don't need the world to tell us what we can do or who we are. All we need is our self, our own permission, and our own acceptance.

I'm not saying this will be easy or that there *will* not be challenges. There *will* be adversity. You will have to continue to strengthen yourself; it's a continual process.

I'm saying it's worth it because it will fill you up. You will feel energized, happy, content – you won't live a drained, run-down, stressed, fatigued life.

Yes, it's possible.

What do you want to receive in your life? Get really clear about your leadership.

What step do you need to take to receive that?

Can you give yourself permission to receive that?

If you can't, you need to work on the belief.

Exercise:

Begin using this mantra – a positive word that you say every day – when you wake up – "I grant myself permission to be

_____."

...*great.*
...*amazing.*
...*successful.*

Choose one. Say it every day. You'll shock yourself how you start to feel uplifted, believing it from the inside out, creating energy that takes away the drained, dead feeling inside.

Though challenging and thought provoking, moving through these leadership questions creates a powerful decision-making process! Authenticity is the process of going back to your origins and *deciding that what makes you happy is worth the work.* It will start you on the path of re-creating the bonds created by the Saboteur. And it will affect how you function in your own life, having a positive impact on the people around you.

You Can Overcome Restrictions

"We feel that you are shackled to fear and self-limiting beliefs. We want you to open your mind to new possibility. Allow the universe to guide you. You are worth it!"

Love, Spirit

How are we restricted as women?

The extreme amount of stress on women, and their ability to handle it all, is beyond my comprehension. As I watched women navigate the world and come into my office ill and exhausted, I realized I had to come up with a plan for them.

I called it Leadership.

If women began to examine Leadership within themselves, I knew they could make different choices, make decisions to influence themselves, put themselves first, and take care of themselves. Receive the possibility that they deserve more than what they're experiencing in their lives.

How could I get women to take different actions in their lives so they can have more energy, more power, more happiness, and more joy to give to their families and their work? Not to mention to themselves! The joy had been sucked out of their lives.

Most leaders know they need certain things in place to get their jobs done: organization, focus, drive, ambition, team, support, community, followers, self-care, money, and peace of mind.

When a woman recognizes her Leadership, she recognizes that her life matters more than the mundane life she's currently leading. She starts to desire more from her life – and asks for it. She physically speaks it to her world, to her relationships, to the people around her.

A leader doesn't hesitate to say, "This is how I want it done. This is the way it needs to be for productivity. This is what I need from you. Get the job done."

Where do we put limitations on ourselves, as women? How do we restrict ourselves, not acting like leaders?

Message From Spirit

In order to get into the heart of your intuitive leadership and your creative passion you will want to cleanse your mind. This does not mean meditating for long hours. It means taking a word, a symbol of truth, and erasing it from your brain with oxygen. As you breathe into the blocks you will erase them. As you write about them you will release them. You have the power to eradicate the blocks standing in your way. Facing your blocks will set you free right now.

The Mind Cleanse is based on years of intuitive guidance and training. I developed it in meditation, during breath-work, and by writing. I developed The Mind Cleanse technique for releasing sabotaging voices and thoughts. Its efficacy relies on two premises:

1. You are energy and your breathing can carry energy. As you breathe you are transmuting the energetic blocks and creating a space for a new state of feeling and intuiting to enter. By energizing a block you are asking it to transform into a more positive feeling. It's like stretching the body. Inside of the inflexible muscle is stored energy potential. Stored within the energetic block and pattern is energy potential. By breathing directly into the block, you will be able to excite it into a new form of flowing energy.

2. Once the block is erased, you have created space for a new energy to enter. You have creative power in this moment. You can replace the block with something better, more positive.

All of the following words are Mind Cleanse words:

Control	*Excuses*	*Restrictions*
Resistance	*Blame*	*Criticism*
Denial	*Limitations*	*Projection*
Avoidance	*Doubt*	*Judgment*

You can place a word like *Restrictions* on what I like to call "the ethereal blackboard". Vision the negative, harmful word with your eyes closed. And then breathe deeply while your mind erases it. Once it is gone, fill the remaining blank space with positive feeling. Describe what you feel.

Flip the Pattern

Please remember that none of this is our fault. It is patterning that must be shifted.

Denial: Women deny personal life force: self-care, nurturance, and support. We're not taking the time to find out who we are and what we really *need* from our life. We are too busy doing it *all*. This pattern shows up in our businesses: we don't delegate or ask for support, *and* we deny ourselves financial flow and prosperity in the wake of that. We are tired, worn out, and unable to manifest. Our light has burned out.

We have programmed self-limiting beliefs that tell us we're not good enough, we don't deserve it, and that it's not possible to think big. We keep ourselves stuck.

Message From Spirit

Spirit showed me this message many times. Women deny themselves love and value...all the time. More over women make excuses, avoid, and blame. It's an epidemic. And it needs fixing by flipping the denial to the other side of the story. Spirit shows me in my practice that there is an urgency to shift this pattern.

The Other Side of Denial: Denial is a story that has appeared because we put power in the hands of the few rather than accept power in ourselves to facilitate life change. Female Leadership creates the space for connection and receptivity, taking time to receive internal answers. That's what stops denial. The opposite of denial is **making decisions** and **having choice**. To do that, we have to stop being a victim and create new decisions even when an authority figure says, "No way". We say, "Yes way!"

Once we're done denying ourselves access to possibility, we then excuse ourselves.

Excuses: Women come into my office with a veritable scroll of reasons (excuses) of why they cannot do something to create life change. I'd see them excuse themselves for the things they wanted, needed, or wanted. Why? Because, it's easier to suffer, and it's *easier* to be the martyr than it is to ask for what you want.

Women excuse greatness, excuse power, excuse decisions and excuse taking health into our own hands. We have given our power away to outside governance.

The inner program we are living tells us we are not worth it, so why even try bothering to practice new things?

These are neurological patterns passed along as generational stressors. Excuses are stories we tell ourselves – and they take us back to our Martyr so we can be of service to others while not receiving for ourselves. That leads us to the pattern of avoiding. We give, however we do not equally receive in return.

The Other Side of Excuses: You have the creative space to be real with what needs to be received to facilitate greater awareness of personal power, even when it is uncomfortable to feel or push through the transformation.

Creative space to receive is the opposite of excusing yourself from the picture of power. Create time for the necessary changes that must happen for deep inner healing and self-worth to take hold. Female intuition asks us to be real with what we are feeling rather than excuse ourselves from feeling and push it underneath our layers of stress. Feel your value, feel your self-worth, feel you power, these are new and important patterns that undo the damage of excuses.

Avoidance: In watching these behavioral patterns, I realized that women were avoiding the truth. We're taught to avoid the pain, emotions, and what's inside of us because it seems to be easier. 'If I can shove these things aside, I can get everything done.' What we don't realize is that by shoving it down, we prolong the agony of dealing with it, which is what we're forced to do when life falls apart, which at some point it will.

As a doctor of preventative medicine, I saw that we held so much emotional baggage and it manifested in sickness and stress. I knew that if I could get my patients to dump it – deal with it and face it – (basically, gain awareness of it) this was the fast, effective path to health, wellness, abundance, and success.

Avoidance prolongs the inevitable: someday, you're going to have to face "it": whatever "it" is bugging you.

What I've learned is how durable the nervous system is and how long we can hang onto hiding. Then, all of a sudden, something happens to you and what's bothering you is exposed. A husband cheats on you. A boss fires you. A parent dies. A child become very ill.

The Other Side of Avoidance: Female Leadership asks the mind to become highly aware and focused on solutions, opportunities for change, and is willing to participate in life change. Female intuition leads us in a positive direction and asks for abundant perception to be created and valued from the inside out. In this form of leadership there is no avoiding. There is focused action on taking power back from negative and self-limiting belief systems that hold us stuck. In Female Leadership, we look at ourselves straight in a clear mirror and show up with a solution to take action and change our behaviors. This means standing up for our internal needs, wants and desires.

And when we're done with avoiding, then we go to blame.

Blame: Now, the "it" has become too big of an issue to fix with a Band-Aid, to hide from, or to shove down. We now have a storm of stuff that is overwhelming. The only thing left for a person to do at this point is dump it on the nearest person, place, or thing.

This blame circuit us really a projection where we play our story onto someone else.

Why is this a problem?

Consider the woman whose husband cheats on her, and she blames the husband and the affair. By then, whatever her "it" was has become such a huge problem in the relationship that the woman is not getting any attention, has no intimacy or sexual flow, so sex is limited, and he goes off to have an affair. Now the blame is on the affair rather than on asking, "Could we have slowed down our life to have connected with each other before this happened?"

But, really, who has the time for connection?

There is also an inner critic inside that blames and projects pain on our self. Perhaps she's blaming herself, too. Women blame themselves because we have a noisy inner critic that perpetuates judgment. We are not good enough, big enough, strong enough, etc. We are just not enough.

How does this keep us stuck? Blame merely perpetuates our pain. It doesn't resolve or transform it – or what caused the pain. In the next relationship, the problem is likely to resurface because the root causes have not been examined.

Start Facing It

Female Leadership takes responsibility for change and asks us to look at all challenges as positive influencers of Inner Strength. Each situation is in our life not to cast onto someone else but to learn from as a life lesson – and as a generator of purpose and direction. There is a power in Female Leadership that is like no other: responsibility. Taking responsibility for our own life work means asking for help to heal and feel better.

But the stuck is real, apparent, and everywhere for women. Why are we so stuck?

Simply, we have no coping mechanisms. We haven't been dealing with everything all along. We haven't been given tools early enough in life to self-reflect and have self-awareness. We do not accept that we are leaders through inner self-awareness, coaching, and living. So, we live from a place of destructive avoidance.

And the patriarchy has told us to not be emotional. But the core of these issues live in our emotional system, not in our brain. They are inside of us. And in many cases, there is a lot of processing – dialogue – that needs to happen for these human issues to resolve themselves.

Again, the patriarchy squelches this process – it doesn't encourage reflection, discussion, or discourse.

In Female Leadership, there *has* to be space for processing, reflection, discussion, discourse, and self-awareness. We have to take time to heal and feel our way into power. Our existence needs to be welcomed and acknowledged for our leadership to emerge.

This takes time and input. It seems time consuming. But when done from the heart and core of feeling, connection can be quite fast. The processing that women need when done from leadership is clean and clear. It can be direct. And it needs to be community-based, supportive, life-giving, and positive.

It's the remaining in stuck that provides slower progress. Sabotage is slow. In the real world, we still need to accomplish the task, meet the goal, and get the job done. We can't spend all our time stuck in our – and other people's – emotions! There needs to be a balance. When we're looking at excuses, denial, avoidance, and blame, we must to be able to get to the truth and deal with it quickly.

I created *On the Other Side* to move through the immense amount of garbage that humans carry in their souls to activate their Leadership and to move them into action as quickly as possible.

All of these patterns begin and end with **Denial**.

Reflect on this question. And write if you feel compelled. *What am I denying myself access to? And how do I change this?*

The Real Demon Is Denial

We all have tendencies to behave in ways that *restrict* our abundance, to habitually *sabotage* our progress in life, and to stop our evolution are hard-wired within us.

Our tendencies are stuck – and are keeping us stuck – and the only way to get beyond the pain and suffering (and get unstuck) is to become empowered.

Empowerment means believing that we deserve more than our circumstances are giving us. It means believing we are worthy to receive what we want out of life rather than what life merely delivers to us. And it takes a lot of new thinking and energy to believe this way, because most of us are stuck in habitual and draining patterns.

Many of our patterns are derived from things that happened to us in our childhood, things we didn't have control over (because we didn't have a voice in the way we were treated or parented). The *only* way to override these patterns is to make an adult decision and take responsibility to change them. To trust that there is a part of our souls that can access more, create more, and become great.

To override denial, avoidance, excuses, blame, and resistance we need the super power of feminine intuition.

The Answers Are In Your Intuition

"We want you to take time to be present with yourself."

Love, Spirit

Intuition is our ability to tune into the subtle feelings, sensations, and energies inside of and around us.

Intuition only knows how to heal us. It is the part of us that is wired to a higher perspective and knowing. And the fastest path to change our restrictions is through intuition.

Intuition is the fire that burns away the toxic patterns. Intuition is deeper than just a thought: it has the ability to override patterns. Thoughts only take us so far. Intuition is a life changer, a game changer, and a power source.

And for many of us, this power source is untapped, underutilized, and extinguished.

Intuition is thought linked to feeling, and the *feeling* is what moves us to take new action.

Why 'Intuition'?

Why is intuition so important? I mean, we have been taught *not* to use intuition: cut it off, fix it, stop it, halt our feelings. In fact, this has disconnected us from the inner truth of who we are.

Intuitive leadership provides a shift vital to our world, forcing us to slow us down to look at ourselves purposefully. When we do this, we must take responsibility and implement changes to move beyond our stuck, sabotaging behaviors.

Those behaviors limit us, skew our perception, cause judgments, and keep us fixed in a certain position with our blinders on. In that state, we cannot see alternatives or options to move forward.

But when we allow intuition to come into play, it doesn't even know our self-limiting beliefs! It's a totally different navigational system that has no idea that our intellectual and analytical brain has created any self-limiting beliefs!

It's incredible and freeing, actually.

Message From Spirit

Intuition only knows how to create opportunities that connect us with our destiny.

Intuition knows you're great. It knows your gifts, your potential...all the positive things about you.

And it knows how to release the negative – that's why it's an incredible tool for getting out of sabotage.

Unfortunately, we don't trust intuition. Why not? Think of fortune tellers or psychics: their work is perceived as woo-woo, inappropriate, impractical, and too far out.

Instead, consider this: they actually are *tuned in to positive solutions* for life changes. Instead of poo-pooing this intuition idea, consider that intuitives are people who stop long enough to listen and provide options – to themselves and others. What if we might go to them to receive a broader perspective on our lives, helping us face challenges and struggles?

Intuition can lead us forward in life, helping make life better for us.

In order to move beyond sabotage, we must learn to dial in, tune in, and sink in to a new way of listening to life. We don't need a psychic or a fortune teller. And yes, we can do this for our self.

How?

Intuition answers questions that we ask ourselves. It allows us to tap into new possibilities. It's creative and wants us to be creative, finding new solutions.

Exercise:

Let's practice.

Dream big and go back to something in your life that you've always wanted to create but have stopped yourself from doing.

Get still and ask yourself: "What do I want to create that I have not yet created?"

There are 3 ways to tune into intuition:

1. Free write on the answer to this question. It will help you strengthen and channel your intuitive energy.

Exercise (cont'd):

2. Feel it inside of your body. Get still and take a deep breath: where do you *feel*? Maybe you'll see yourself creating the 'something new' or you may feel it as an emotional vibration inside your body. Define that for yourself.

3. Vision the thing you've wanted to create. See yourself in a new way, as if on a movie screen. This is the most difficult way to tune in, so vision boarding can help you.

There is a 4th way to tune into intuition, and though it's more advanced, we all have the capability within us.

4. Use a deeper perspective here called Inner Knowing. You've got a core feeling (if you can get quiet to let yourself feel it) about something. You just know it, and there is no logical thought about it. It's a sensation or a push moving you to do something in your life. When you engage with this, stop pushing it down, and let it move you, *this* is when you'll see incredible momentum happen in your life.

How willing are you to trust your inner voice, your intuition, your inner knowing? You can move beyond the things that stop you from accessing your inner self.

Your nervous system has put up barricades, restrictions, and walls that won't allow you to access your intuition. This book and its exercises are designed to move you through the barricade, remove the restrictions, break down the wall.

If what I've written here is so overwhelming because you have to stop and be with yourself, and this silence may make you uncomfortable, then try the following extra exercise.

In your daily movement through the world (driving, walking, surfing the web), merely ask the universe to show you signs. Say, "Show me what I need to know to advance my life." And then pay attention to what shows up. What is sent to you? Look for numbers, words, symbols, repetitive messages, colors, people, opportunities. They will show up; however, don't force them to happen.

Why Move Into Intuition?

Our Inner Voices cannot not be heard, so we cannot define ourselves with *them*. They've been overtaken by a patriarchal system that has created a box that we are forced to fit into. Let me explain how this works subtly in everyday life, using the topic of physical appearance as an example.

A husband objects to his wife's paint-spattered clothing with a horrified, "What are you wearing!?" She then rushes upstairs to take care of herself and put on her tidy, neat, acceptable clothing. This woman wanted to be creatively working on her house, but her husband wanted a wife who is well-dressed and presentable. He has not even defined what "presentable" means to her, so she is left scrambling to PLEASE an *outside* voice.

Another couple plays with the system in a different way. This wife is dolled up with makeup, clothes, and hair done, but when her husband sees her he says, "How could you look like that? What did you do with yourself?!"

Both women are leaders in their communities, serve on boards, hold leadership positions in companies, parent amazing children, etc. Both women, when they go home, bow down to the masculine domination of who they're defined to be. Neither has any identity at home.

Neither has a voice that is heard. Intuition is a function of LISTENING to inner desire.

A woman in her intuitive power would leave the room, sit down, breathe, and ask, "What do I want? What do I feel? How do I want to dress?" And then walk downstairs in paint spattered clothing to continue her day, if that's what she chose.

Message From Spirit

We need to move into intuition because behavior has also been co-opted. Take the woman who is a leader at home, feels good inside of her body, and knows how to dress for herself. She does not allow her appearance be dictated to her by men. She walks into work with confidence and is financially powerful, gaining some power and influence. She does not doll up to be seen. She does not dress down to hide. She does not shut up to put up. She is a stealth force of inner calm, peace and knowing. A woman who has inner knowing of who she is and why she is here will work extra hard to make sure she stands up for herself.

This woman is the most feared force on the planet, yet must be celebrated.

She is, of course, known as a bitch who has too much power. However, this woman who knows herself inside and trusts it is not affected by the outside chaos and cut downs. She knows how to go to her sisterhood and make sure she processes the cutting remarks and strengthens her inner knowing to stand true to herself in the face of adversity.

How does our 'lack' of intuition and inner knowing manifest? What is the real trouble with it, beyond the ego?

Well, consider the woman who has lost it all. At home, she is controlled by her abusive husband who tells her how to behave and how to dress.

At work, she is subservient and invisible, has no voice or leadership role. She hides in life and has lost her voice. This is the woman who would show up in my chiropractic practice as *physically ill*.

All of these women have lost intuition. Their fire is out. The energy to stand up and say, "I will not take this anymore" dies out in the control they're experiencing.

These women fear change: will they lose their husband, their job, any respect they have? In my experience, women will stay in a traumatic situation because they will lose their financial situation.

However, a woman who is empowered would never consider this. That woman doesn't care if the world sees her as a bitch; she stands up for what she believes is right and is willing to voice her truth and express her emotions.

She has the tough conversations and is willing to deal with the consequences. She is willing to show up and represent herself – who she is with strength – without fear or apology.

You can be this woman, too. One of the key, driving factors to achieving it is *learning to get in touch with your intuitions*.

Exercise

Develop **HER** Intuition.

Start opening intuition in your brain. Focus your energy on the question, "What do I want?" Only you can answer the question, "Is what I'm dealing with right now – and the potential shit I'm dealing with – really worth it?" Use the Play Big mentality and stretch higher in your thoughts.

HEAD: Get your head focused on your wants. To answer this question, deeply engage with this question and do a want cleanse.

Exercise (cont'd):

I want _____ .

I want _____ .

I want _____ .

This is your work. Write up to 25 or 30 "I want _____ " statements. As you drill down into them and let them fall into the paper, you're making space for your intuitions

EMOTION: Evoke a feeling from your heart about your wants. Feelings will tune you in to sensations which will open intuition.

Re-read your list of wants. As you review them, something will evoke emotions. The ones that matter the most, the ones that will turn into your intuition, will leap off the page at you, causing your heart to engage. I promise, you'll see it in a different way.

Perhaps share it with a friend who doesn't judge you. Which ones excite you? Cause you to feel *feeling?* Feel hot, angry, excited, upset? Circle these. Highlight these. Then move them into the Receptivity Zone.

RECEPTIVITY = Intuition. These are the wants you want to receive into your life to make your life better. They feel the most powerful and move you forward, causing action.

Whittle down your list of the wants to the ones that evoked emotion, and pick the one that you respond to with the strongest emotion.

Develop holding power with it. Hold it as a new thought. Write it on a piece of paper and put it on your mirror. Journal about it. Say it out loud to yourself. Roll it around in your brain and think about what life would be like with this intuition coming to fruition.

This is the beginning of the breakthrough of denial. When we ask ourselves to receive our intuitions we are igniting a change from the inside out.

We are saying, "I want to live a different life. I *deserve* more than this. I *deserve* more than being called a 'bitch' or 'aggressive'. I *deserve* to lead from my true authentic power. I *deserve* more than my husband telling me what to wear or what to say."

This work requires energy, sisterhood, and collaboration. We have been so beaten down, so lost our voice, that the work is tough to do. You need a buddy system. Work through these blocks with a spiritual guide, friend or coach.

Activate Your Intuition By Facing Denial

The questions to ask at this point is, "What do I want beyond my denial? What's on the other side of my denial for me?" For example, I see over and over a denial of *help*. Are you denying yourself the help, support, and collaboration you need to build a powerful business, family life, and happiness?

Once you have journaled and talked about exactly what you are denying, you can easily create the opposite polarity. And once you are able to create *that* definition, you are able to move toward it with action steps of self-reflection and self-awareness.

Exercise:

Journal with the following questions to get there.

1. **What are you denying yourself?**
   I'm denying myself help. Help with the children.
   Help with marketing. Help with cleaning. Whatever it is.

2. **What do I want? What is my intuition?**
   Someone to pick up my kids each day after school.
   A marketing team. A cleaning lady.

3. **What are the self-limiting beliefs that pop up when I ask for what I want?**
   Identify these Rebel Voices: I can't afford this.
   I don't deserve this. I should be able to do it all.
   Why can't I handle all of this.

4. **How do you want to take action?**
   Use the self-limiting belief, or step into the bigger action and activate (make happen) what you want and need.

   a. Use the beliefs: journal, reflect, and ultimately release. And then take action.

   b. Activate: go out and just get the thing you need.

As you activate your intuition and begin to practice and participate with trusting, the ugly monster of DOUBT will surface. It is a part of our sabotage system that keeps us stuck, keeps us from "knowing."

Overcome Doubt

"As you tune into intuition and develop your intuitive power, your doubts will surface as a Rebel Voice. We are here to help you overcome doubt and TRUST. Trust the flow of intuitive information."

Love, Spirit

What if, what if, what if…

What if no one shows up?
What if you fall on your face?
What if this is another failure?

When we focus only on the 'what ifs', doubt arises. This leads to paralysis. Doubt is the brain saying stay safe. It is an old safety mechanism that needs an override. What's the antidote?

Strategy.

Strategy overrides doubt. We have to build a strategy, an action plan that puts into motion what it is we want to achieve from life.

How specific does a strategy have to be? Well, it has to be specific enough to motivate us to act. Actions steps help us overcome the things that hold us back. They rewrite the sabotaging patterns!

Be warned: sometimes we create strategies that restrict or paralyze us. We resist moving forward. It's our way of pushing back, saying, "Oh, no. I'm not going to change. I cannot change. This is the way it is and this is the way I know it."

How does resistance keep us in doubt? It tells us, "You're safer if you stay where you are. What you've got is working for you well enough right now. There's no need to change! Why would you want to change the world? Why would you want to..."

What if, what if, what if...?

Melanie is a gifted speaker who doubts that she can make it into speaking. She has designed a very tight, structured, and strategized existence as a *fantastic* high school teacher. Her daily strategy is to get up and teach history as a speaker. She motivates and inspires kids, giving them an authentic voice. She holds resistance and doubt around whether she can take this gift and ability to the next level and stage.

Can she empower other women and teachers, sharing her story of how she's overcome adversity and learned to live an authentic life on purpose?

I know she absolutely CAN, but she *only* sees herself as a teacher. She is highly structured in her strategy to be the best teacher, and ultimately this keeps her in doubt *and* from achieving the next level of her leadership.

The strategy you create to change your leadership to align with your purpose must be stronger than what you've developed in the past or what has (or hasn't) worked up until this point.

You have to feel it from the inside out as a mission. It moves through you and expresses itself as a true part of who you are. It's an inner-knowing, a certainty, a knowing that you can do this.

For Melanie, she already knows what she does on a daily level: her transformational speaking works *every single day* in the classroom. However, she is feeling boxed in, limited, restricted, financially maxed out, mundane, and boring. However, she is really good at teaching and passionate about inspiring others. She feels that from the inside out. She knows she can motivate people; she knows she can speak.

What is holding her back? Doubt, fear, and worry are all collaborating to create resistance to her taking the next step.

What is her next step? What is her strategy?

Many mistake "strategy" for "a to-do list" or a "getting the degree/ certification". Strategy is really about just becoming a more-improved version of who you are and growing beyond the boundaries we've put in place.

Ok, so what should Melanie do to implement an effective strategy that will overcome her doubt?

It's simpler than she thinks it is: take action.

The doubt fear and worry want to make the process complex. They make it twisted and convoluted.

Instead, the question becomes, 'What can I do today - outside of this mundane environment - to emerge the quality I know I have inside me?'

Are you noticing the opportunities that could pull you away from the mundane environment? The opportunities that could actually *feed* your emerging qualities?

We doubt our true potential all the time. We put up walls and create reasons why we cannot do it, when in fact, the world is dropping innumerable opportunities in front of us that will feed us.

Jen felt absolutely dead inside. She was running a business that didn't feed her dream, even though she was incredibly good at it. For a long time, Jen told herself that being good at this job was enough. It was what she was supposed to do. She would let everyone down if she left. So, she stayed and slowly died inside.

She says, "There was a moment where I realized I was bringing everyone down with me. My deadness was contagious. I couldn't live with that – I didn't want to feel dead for myself, but certainly not for my husband and family. I didn't even recognize myself anymore. I had scripted myself into [my business] so tightly that I was suffocating myself, the business, my relationships, my family."

Does your family feel as dead as you do?
Does your business feel as dead as you do?
Are your partners as dead as you are?
Are your customers as dead as you are?

You are hurting the people around you, and more so, *you are hurting yourself*. This is not what a leader does; or - to be clearer – this is ineffective leadership.

The severity of doubt is incredible: doubt is a liar.

Melanie's doubt is lying to her. And it's stopping her. It's causing suffering because she's not living an authentic life – she is trapped in the box, tied to the ball and chain of what she "should" be doing and what a woman "could" do. These stories don't match her inner truth and destiny. If you met her in real life, you'd know it in a second. This strategy of hers might have been part of her productive past, but it isn't part of her evolutionary strategy of change, growth, and excellence.

She feels muted inside.

To become alive again – and affect others around her positively (in other words, becoming a leader) – she needs an effective strategy:

Strategy 1: Find someone who sees her. Or, notice the opportunities dropped in her path to see herself in a different light. NOTICE. If you cannot notice them yourself, then you can hire someone to do this – a coach, a therapist, a personal trainer, a strategist, consultant. Allow yourself to be seen in your gifts and valued.

Strategy 2: Realize inside of her that she has an amazing potential to transform other people. She is doing this via self-examination, journaling, and energy medicine. She became self-reflective.

Strategy 3: Become self-accepting, seeing herself as powerful. She has to learn to accept her negative and positive aspects. Love the positive and heal the negative – let go of self-negating thoughts and clear the path to speak.

Strategy 4: Do it. Get up on the stage and strengthen the inner speaker. SPEAK. Take any and every opportunity.

Strategy 5: Do it again. And again. And again, until it's like breathing.

Basically, this process develops creative energy, a life-force that gives you power – removing the self-limiting beliefs, limiting situations, stifling energy that kills your life force.

The only way to heal this is to create the situation you want in your life by knowing who you are from the inside out. Have you done that work yet?

Exercise:

Doubts. Worries. Fears.

How can you erase them from your life, letting them go?

1. Recognize the negative pattern.

   - Create three separate papers and label them Doubt, Worry and Fear.

   - Write down the negative thoughts that fit into each category.

   - Rip it up and throw it away. Burn it.

Exercise (cont'd):

2. What do you want to create?

    - Imagine yourself as a creator having the power to make something happen. State it. Write it down. Draw it. Imagine it. Say it out loud. "I want to create myself into a motivational speaker."

    - Ask yourself, "How am I going to do this? What are the actions I need to take to become a motivational speaker?" Focus on this creative energy: write the answers down and focus on the ones that are the "low hanging fruit", so to speak. Which ones are do-able, which ones are opportunities that speak to my authentic purpose? What's most accessible?

    - Then you take the opportunity, *knowing you'll be terrified, knowing you're not going to be perfect, and noticing how you feel when you're doing it.*

How can you surge and grow THAT feeling – the feeling of incredible freedom and happiness when you've taken the opportunity that's landed in front of you!

You have to lead to change your life. Leadership is the only thing that will heal you from this mundane, restrictive environment. It is the ONLY thing that will turn on your life force.

Community Is The Fast Forward of Change

"We want you to work your intuitive process together, as a community of light and love. This is the fastest path to change and the world needs supportive groups of collaborative, open, and honest change."

Love, Spirit

How do you create intuition for real change? Throughout the pages of this book you may have turned over a new leaf.

You may have decided to focus on the female form of leadership.

You may have started to decide that you are a leader.

You may have seen that you *can* make leadership decisions and your life can improve.

You may have a greater sense of awareness over your blocks and patterns of stuck.

You may be able to recognize the Saboteur and the Rebel Voices.

You may have even made a decision to stop doubting yourself, move beyond fear, and create more life force and power in your business and life.

But, where does the change happen? How can you develop a stronger relationship with your feminine power?

I have discussed that you are intuitive. That you have an inner knowing that is much stronger than the sabotaging patterns and limiting beliefs. That access to your inner intuition will fast forward you beyond blocks and move you into purpose and destiny.

Intuition is the power to help you attract great wealth and achieve new success.

This process of leadership and overcoming your blocks may seem overwhelming and a task that is impossible to accomplish. I want to tell you it is *totally* possible to step into your star power and live from a more multidimensional approach to life. Believe that there *are* possibilities that you never have imagined.

And as you begin to flatten the hierarchy in your mind and see yourself as a spiritual being with purpose and destiny, you can access a part of your feminine spirit that *has to lead.*

You are a spiritual beam of light for the world. What you think, how you feel and what you are going through matters. You are influential and impactful. And the ideas you've generated for your business and life are powerful tools for advancing the world.

To make the impact you were designed to create, you have to once again begin to believe in your self-worth. And the path to this belief is through intuition.

There is an entire energy system inside of you that can be accessed and utilized for your life and business advancement. When you begin to intuitively strengthen your presence, you will realize that you have a divine birthright to access the positive flow of your feminine power so you can live an abundant life.

I do not say this because I am making it up. I have lived this process and opened to my own feminine flow of power and presence. I went from no purpose to an incredible destiny of teaching women leadership and intuitive power. And I feel that it is through our energetic body and inner knowing of destiny that we will be able to fast forward beyond the stuck and begin to rise up to a level of impact where our vision of a healthy, happy world can be heard and validated.

No matter how intuitive or vision-driven a man might be, he still *needs* our creative power: the masculine needs the feminine to balance out the extremes. Men still need our collaborative and creative power to help the world become a better place.

The masculine needs the feminine. And it is our responsibility to bring this to the world.

So how can we do this in the fastest way possible? And why do we need speed?

Speed and agility is necessary right now because we are at a crossroads, what many spiritualists are calling a shift in consciousness. This shift in consciousness is necessary and is part of our human awakening to abundance, love, and spirit.

Yet, in this awakening there is also a huge amount of suffering, pain, hatred, and kickback from the density, the heaviness. Thus, we need speed and agility, which comes from a clear channel through our energy body and into creative power.

The channel that needs to be opened will be demonstrated in my next book, but for now I will teach you about manifesting your destiny through 8 steps that can help you become a spiritual woman with a leadership purpose. A process I call The 8 Steps for Transformation.

I feel like the biggest project for *On the Other Side* is to open to our spiritual power, intuitive sense, and manifesting flow. Then and only then can we fast forward beyond the blocks that are in our system.

My Story Collaborate and Circle

Where did this process of intuitive opening occur?

It was back in my 1st Wellness Office that I received my own divine message to start a feminine circle.

But in 2002 we did not have internet in my office. I did not have a website; it was too costly. Social media was nowhere to be found.

In fact, my space was the only way to connect. I needed fast and effective ways to open people up and connect women to the limitless potential of healing trough innate intelligence.

Being intuitive, I listened to the voices and feelings that directed me to connect with people in new ways. And a voice directed me to create a circle of transformation for women. They also told me to charge what I thought to be a ridiculous amount at that time. However, as a good student of spirit I listened and I charged $1000 for a program.

I tell you this because it was a very progressive step to go from $100-per-hour sessions to a circle of women paying $1000 for a program.

By listening to intuition I began my own personal study of female community, collaboration, and circle. And I used this process to build the energetic program I will introduce to you as the final chapters of this book.

I wanted to move women out of their box and into their potential.
I wanted women to connect with spirituality and awakening.
I wanted to bring women together to facilitate transformation.

It was innate for me, part of my destiny, to facilitate a circle. I had no formal training, no credentials, no position to create the circle for empowering women. I just knew intuitively how it was to be done. And, this is still true to this day in all of my programs.

Moving from a box (the shut up and put up model) into a circle (let's process your junk so that you can move forwards faster) worked via a Leadership Circle to flatten hierarchy and create a feminine model.

We've put people in a box, and we've asked them to stay there – as a world. The paradigm has been 'control and dominate women, then put them in a self-limiting container.' We learn through school and families to be quiet, turn off our power, be silent, not be seen, to hold back, to keep our feelings to ourselves, to hold our tears in, and to shut down our creativity.

I was tired of it.

In my business as a Chiropractor, a woman creating a wellness facility and woman-owned business, I made the decision to create a feminine model of leadership and business. There was a thought that went through me that "I'm going to run this like a woman would." That means – to me, I was going to run it from my intuition and the way I wanted to. I didn't even know what this meant, but I knew I didn't want to run it the way the way other businesses had been run. I was looking at how other women were running their lives.

I said no to putting my kids in daycare. I said no to leaving my kids and running a business and stressing myself out – running myself down and not having anything for them.

I wanted to have enough to give my family.

The business model I'd studied in chiro school did not resonate with me. I didn't have a model – there were pieces I liked – but these business development models I'd seen were not giving me what I needed.

Ultimately what I needed was:

1. To be a healthy leader. To love myself in the process. Self-care and nurturance must be part of my business model. I refused to lose the work I'd already done to create self-love because I wanted to start a business. Other women I saw were stressed out, sick, and depleted – just holding it together – barely able to give anything to their families.

2. To have my kids with me: my family would be well-cared for with a present mom (not a perfect mom).

3. Money-driven: to have a lucrative practice and be well taken care of financially.

If I could get these 3 pieces to work together, I felt I'd have the full picture.

I asked my inner guide for the first step, and the answer I received was to create a collaborative community. I had no idea where to start, however I began to create facilitated community groups and workshops. These were unique spaces where women could be heard, process emotions, and grow together.

I figured that when women came together with the same intention, answered the same questions and worked together as a collective mindset that exponential change could happen. I created a facilitated workshop for women to fully express themselves and feel supported and safe in their healing process.

As I began to create community inside of my Chiropractic office, I trained my staff (both men and women) to become part of the circles, bringing it into my business as a place for people to voice what they were feeling on the job and grow into better employees. It also gave them the ability to understand and empathize with clients. It was a relationship-building tool for clients and staff.

The process of facilitated community was designed to create a collaborative healing and life-change space to help women move beyond stuck and sabotage into empowered living.

I created:

1. Common ground: neutral space for working through stuck patterns.

2. Heightened awareness through community: we were able to advance by learning from each other's transformations.

3. A place to build relationships with people.

I designed a curriculum for staff training that became the foundation of my wellness center operations. The ultimate goal was to have employees express themselves, to have a voice inside their jobs. That made them more dedicated to their purpose within that organization. I wanted to create a community where people would thrive.

Two things happened: I created the collaborative transformation community that was the foundation for all of my trainings and simultaneously made it into a business model, empowering staff to move the business forwards with me, as a team.

I leveled the playing field, taking the hierarchy out of the business. My staff and renters saw me as the leader, but they had a strong voice in how the business could be directed. Therefore, they had a sense of ownership of the business. We worked together to help our customers and clients feel welcome, happy, supported, and joyful as they went through our transformative services.

The community collaboration has an internal strategy to emerge the leadership in every person – which means they become willing and able to take responsibility for their own thoughts and actions. That is what creates unity and cohesiveness. When a person is deep in stuck behaviors and habits, they can learn from others in the group how to progress. And even when people have differing viewpoints, the business moves congruently because everyone is on the same page.

I realized when I empowered my employees and renters, it made my job easier. We had an open and honest space to dialogue, work through issues and connect.

When I built my 2nd wellness center, I started calling it Leadership Circle. Calling it a "Healing Circle" kept people in suffering, focused on their wounds. Leadership focused them on moving forwards and evolving, strengthening their purpose.

The masculine model – hierarchical and in a box – keeps us controlled. In it, there is one voice and minimal input to one's own power. There is an idea that when things are stacked in that hierarchical model, things can be controlled in a top-down manner. Orderly, silo-ed, with one voice given to a number of people. Everyone is supposed to fall in line and follow that – and if a person doesn't agree, that person is wrong.

The collaboration model empowers everyone to have his or her own ideas and work together to achieve one common goal – this goal is of the organization. But this circle allows everyone to work together to achieve the goal.

In the fast pace of life, this seems to be a slower path because you have to wait for processing, but that is a false belief. When facilitated and guided by a skilled communicator with a solid program, the group cohesiveness actually moves people through stuck perceptions and unwillingness to change FASTER than hierarchy.

Message From Spirit

Collaboration Moves Faster

Why is this true? Because people learn to work together and play on each other's strengths, learning from each other. There is a facilitated state of acceptance and greatness.

How? A leadership collaboration program understands that the facilitated leader has created the goal: this person is both a facilitator and a participant. She is not going to tell you what to do or say or feel, but is going to engage with her own empowerment process and grow along with everyone else.

This is a position that holds respect and honor: this person has knowledge, and all the participants realize that they can buy into the agenda and the purpose (or they don't, and they realize they are in the wrong place/job).

That's why people in the circle will engage authentically.

The business owner/leader/etc. must create the goal or intention. It's still their business. The circle doesn't take away titles or positions: it just gives people the opportunity to communicate their commitment and dedication to the overall goal of the organization. It's a connector circuit: connecting them into an effective community, giving them the sense of belonging. When people feel like they belong, they will do anything for you.

That's why it's faster.

It's amazing what can get done when we ask people to collaborate in an intuitive way, try to achieve a common goal, with clear communication. We actually get shit done.

The power of intention is vital: the Circle Leader brings the intention of collaboration to the circle. The intention is delivered to the circle; people are given the space and time to think about and feel the intention.

For instance, the topic may be client relations. A question is put out and each participant gets to think, write, and then share his or her voice about this topic in the current moment.

The 2nd question might be how do we improve client relations? We need improvements...here is what's happening...so how do we do that? The circle members get the opportunity to share insights, perspectives, and ideas to solve the problem.

By listening to the ideas of everyone in that circle, we allow all the ideas to be filtered – and the decision maker (facilitator) gets to say, "I like what's been presented today, and I am going to use this to help our company move forward."

The age of technology and the masculine model has stripped the human aspect from business. This model will only work if you believe that your business is a community and your community has a purpose and an impact to make. It will only work if you want to create a humanistic approach to business.

Is this for everyone? Absolutely not. Not every business is here to help humans advance. Those based on treating people with kindness and respect would benefit from investing in the time and great effort it takes to insert a leadership circle model into their business.

The outcome is a faster, more efficient way to create customer service circuit: customer service, client, and business. There's a relationship that fluidly runs between all those elements. It's the opposite of a model of domination and control. This model creates room for the authentic self. It reduces disruption and distraction. It focuses people on an ultimate goal and outcome. It motivates them to move toward the same direction.

It's the opposite of silos. It's the opposite of cubicles.

Why do we take the self-expression of humanity out of our lives? Why are we dulling ourselves? Why do we think that getting people together is a waste of time?

OPEN YOUR SPIRIT CHANNEL

The 8 Steps of Transformation

"We decided to give you a program that would open your channel for you to receive our messages. This program is simple to use and easy to follow and when done in community can have amazing, radical results. We want you to practice intuitive transformation."

Love, Spirit

Community To Transformation

I began to study how women transformed much faster in community while using intuition. I recognized patterns and solutions to these patterns that are all part of this book.

And I realized that most women needed a structured solution to open the channel of intuitive and receive downloads for their own destined progress in the world. I also learned through facilitating circles that when women were placed in a spiritual and energetic environment they immediately flourished.

And by studying with the women in circle, I began to devise my own integrative program for helping women open connection to higher self-guidance and intuition. I realized that if women were going to change that we needed a system and community of change to get the job done.

What follows in the next 8 steps is a review of the program I now use to open the channel of intuition so that women can learn to listen to destiny. And they can give birth to amazing programs and projects that will impact world change.

Transformation To Intuition

I knew in my heart that women needed to reach higher for desire and access dreams. I wanted to help women descend dreams into reality and manifest immediate results. It was my understanding that women could do this by descending spiritual insights through energy centers of the body that had been wired to the nervous system.

Although its seemed crazy I knew that energetically when women connected with intention and breath, they could achieve amazing results.

As a healer and manifestation guru I decided to use the chakras to manifest immediate results. The intuitive pathways that women needed were wired to these energy centers, and I knew they would produce fast results for transforming women into leaders of action.

The Chakras

After reading about the stuck and sabotage, you are probably wondering what the bleep? If life is so dismal how do I get beyond this power struggle of man vs. woman and negative vs. positive?

To keep it simple, here's what you need to know: the chakras are energy centers that hold information about your past, present, and future life. They are fueled by energy from your nervous system in the form of nerve plexus. The energy flows off the nerves and energizes the chakras. Each chakra has a story or meaning to tell based on the posture of the body.

Each chakra has a meaning symbolically to a woman's life, so I designed 8 steps to help women work with the chakras in a very practical way. The goal is to open the intuitive body for inner knowing. I felt that the more open a woman could become to her chakra descent, the better her life could become. I called this path Dream to Reality or Destiny to Reality.

As you begin to work with the symbolic energy of each chakra and bring the energy into alignment, your entire body can reorganize itself around the positive energy. You will flow with light and love rather than negativity.

As women connect with positive rather than negative, they can fast-forward beyond the negative and stuck into a more practical approach to living from destined truth and professional power.

The more women engage with mission and purpose, the greater impact they have on world change. I want to create a huge impact on people and change, and I found that this path, the one I am revealing here, is one of the most powerful avenues to impact.

Over and over in my healing and coaching, I see that every woman needs more positive energy poured into life in a very structured and systematic way. It is like pouring water into a dried-up sponge: the water is soaked up and absorbed very quickly. Women need positive intention in the form of intuition and we need it quickly.

Positive energy is something that needs practice and repetition. It is a "muscle" that needs strengthening. And through the 8 steps, women can open to the fact that they matter *more* than the negativity, the stuck, and the sabotage.

I fully believe that in the structure of the chakras, we open to our higher guidance. Each and every woman has been put here to open up and receive the destiny and purpose to help the world change. This may show up by reshaping your attitude, helping guide a relationship, running a multimillion dollar company, or via the power of passion and pleasure. No matter what you do with this system, you will open to your intuition on many levels, engage your positive energy to overcome sabotage, and move beyond the stuck four walls of your life.

And the more positive a female leader becomes in intent, visions, presence, and action, the better it is for everyone in her life. Energy multiplies and grows quickly and efficiently. The ability to see, feel, and act from the positive is the catalyst for life change that can shift the world in a more healthy, happy and prosperous direction.

So how do you open up to receive messages? How do you take the time you need to bust through the limiting thoughts and behaviors described in the past chapters that wall you off from your real self?

There has to be an opening in your schedule. A place and time for you to do a reality check into where you are today and what you want. I have created 8 simple steps for you to master your intuition, begin to listen at different levels of consciousness, and receive data and input from your higher self.

It will take time and practice to become more self-aware, however the fun part is that you can begin to bypass the stuck and sabotage in your life by channeling the higher self-wisdom you were born to achieve.

Your journey begins with the first step.

8 Steps To Overcome Sabotage And Transform

Step 1: The Check In
What are your thoughts today? In this present moment, what is happening right now in my life? What needs to come out? This brings us into our present moment (i.e. work, home, kids, colleagues, partner, etc.) and connects us with the reality of our life *in this moment* right now. The Right Now is the only place that change can happen! Step 1 is the most important step because it puts words and thoughts and feelings to the moments of our lives – which reveal the things we need to work through.

Step 2: The Higher Self
What do you want your thoughts to be? This is where we rise above the chaos, pain, and loss to look at things from a higher perspective. The easiest way to find this space is to polarize where are we today with what we ultimately want. If where I am today is, "I'm in pain", then my polar

opposite is, "I want to be out of pain." We cannot have our ultimate pleasure without examining our troubles of today. We can only know where we're going– or where we want to go – if we examine where we are today. What's shitty today?

Step 3: Seeing is Believing

Can you see what you want? Most people skip over this part. Our intuition and perception is stuck; our ability to describe what we want by being able to see it is broken. When we see something happen in front of our own eyes, it creates a place of *allowing*, bringing to life what was once just a thought. When it starts to animate, our imagination opens up so we can move beyond sabotage. Imagine life being better! Imagine pain going away! Imagine people being kinder! This steps sheds light on the new path we want to take, freeing stuck energy – and life becomes happier. This step informs and guides us very deeply about who we are and why we're here.

Step 4: Speaking It

Can you speak about what you want? Connect with deep desires by sending words into the world. These words are a signal that connect with reality and bring our desires into the practical world. Speaking is one of the most connective forms of manifesting what we want. Ironically, we are often afraid to speak what we want because it often *brings it into reality*. Practicing speaking what we want regularly changes the tone of our voice and works on our soul. The more we speak from our higher self, the more our voice changes and becomes truthful. People with a hard time speaking what they want often whisper or squeak. With practice speaking about what we want *over time,* we see a change in our voice. It gets deeper, more articulate, more resonant, with clearer, more defined words.

Step 5: Feeling It

What do you feel? As our words create resonance, they create a pathway to the heart of connection. Now we're starting to be real with our life, and our heart starts to open, allowing *feeling* (positive or negative). These sensations – what we feel in our heart – are a truthful reality. It's a level of honesty that many of us need to sink into in order to move through sabotage. Our heart space knows the truth, but our walls have been up, keeping the energy locked from the other side of our truth. This is a habitual pattern that we have been trained to engage in, and this work unlocks that.

Step 6: Empower It

How is this feeling giving me power? Feeling is fuel for the flame of power. Power is a natural by-product of feeling. Women have created a misperception that, "I'm energetic and vital when I'm walled off", but our energy lives in our feelings. And as we get real with those feelings, it creates movement inside our energy body – which creates REAL energy. How this gives us power is to give direction to that energy. Here is where we find our mission. Examples: "I feel angry, so this is about releasing what no longer serves my body" or "I feel joy, and I need to plug this joy into creating more clients for my business." Ask, "When I feel this way, how does this empower my life?" When we allow ourselves to feel the full spectrum of emotion –positive and negative – and really process that, it turns into pro-active action.

Step 7: Move It

How can I take action? Accessing the feelings and creating a mission from it in Step 6 feeds and informs the action steps. This step is designed around your higher self-interest. We've moved through and dropped down into the body, and now we can ask, "What do I need to do?". Here, we know that we're doing the things – taking the actions – that serve our highest and best selves. These steps move us through stuck and sabotage and are difficult at first. We must keep going and have faith that we are moving down our life's path.

Step 8 Become It

Who am I becoming? This is where we change, shift, and grow. Surprise! Here we see we've become a new person. What we've learned in the 8 steps is that we must walk through difficult emotions, sensations, and communications to get to the new self that we wanted to be. Here, we may crack the door open and peek at who we might become. We see that we are powerful. Smart. Beautiful. Begin to accept the real, honest truth of who we are and why we are here.

These are integrative steps that build on each other, creating an energy that causes us to actually feel different as women; the Female Leadership system works synergistically to knock down the walls created earlier in our lives. Working all of these steps creates a *collaborative* energy system inside the body to break down walls keeping us stuck. When we engage, we move to the other side of the story. This is where we begin to live the life we really want.

The 8-step intuitive journey takes you through your body and represents a powerful connection to your creative power. By coming into alignment with all seven of your chakras, you amp up your inner intelligence and divine healing power. This also sets into motion your destiny and creative life path.

As you work through these steps and transform your own life and profession, you will begin to open to more, allow more love, and believe that you can receive greatness in your life. You will begin to see clearly how you are part of a big picture of awakening.

And you have an important part to play in helping to heighten the conscious connection on the planet.

The 8 steps are here to teach you that *you hold the creative power*. The more you focus on the power of positive creativity, the more abundant your life will become.

I want you to live an amazing life of empowerment. The creative process is all you. It is your authentic birthright to own. And you now have insight into the tools to manage your ability to create what you want in symphony with both your higher- and lower-self guiding your footsteps.

As you work with each of the positive steps in this process you will begin to understand that the power of the simple yet profound exercises presented within this book are a gateway for people who may be trapped in doubtful, hopeless and desperate situations. With the simplicity of the steps above, you *can* transform, heal, and lead from a positive place of love.

Message From Spirit
We love you. Thank you!

FINAL THOUGHTS AND OFFERINGS

On the Other Side is a combination of channeled messages and clinical information.

⁓ⱻ⅌⅌ⱻ⁓

The book is a spiritual coaching program designed to help you see that there is more to life than you have been experiencing. When you can see on the other side of your life and discover that big ideas and visions can be downloaded to reality through spirit, you will break down the walls of resistance and use intuition as a guide.

This shift will help you advance your life. And as you learn to broaden your perspective your life and life will become high performance.

It is my ultimate goal to help you open your channel and receive the guidance you truly deserve, so the universe can conspire in your favor and work with you.

As a leader, speaker and facilitator I talk to people all the time about intuitive messages from spirit. My medium practice is full and alive with messages that I channel to help people achieve greatness in life and business. My facilitated programs help people all over the world connect with source power to breakthrough to lasting change.

My mission is to create sustainable change by applying the science of intuition and energy medicine. I believe that as we learn to channel and open to spirit, we become energy conduits that surge positive vibes of love and positive transition on the planet. The system you find in this book, guided by universal forces, has important strategy.

I have an amazing career where I get to train spiritual leaders from the heart and soul of change and inspiration. And, I invite you to join me.

I believe that our intuition and connection to the universe is the fast forward through stuck and pain and can guide us to an amazing life filled with love. Spiritual channeling is the pathway out of sabotage and into a life filled with opportunity and abundance.

My channeling system is devised to help you open up your spiritual powers. In my books and trainings I will teach you how to listen to higher guidance, follow what is being shown to you, and use guidance as a system for navigating life. I will validate your process and help you trust that you can channel REAL information through higher connection.

My programs and services offer a wide array of opportunity to connect with spiritual understanding and energy medicine. We support individuals and organizations in their quest to achieve amazing change.

Products and Services Offered:

Performance Coaching for Actors

Business Coaching Services

Medium and Intuitive Consulting

Advanced Energy Training

Spiritual Channeling and Medium Events

To learn more about Dr. Pam and her services go to **www.PamDenton.com**.

Have Dr. Pam Denton Speak To Your Group!

The Spirit of Leadership

Pam's speaking and training is designed for Power on Demand (PODs): filling up and accessing your personal tank with energy, creativity, motivation, and transition. Power on Demand means you want change to happen now so that you can create what you want in your life. Pam asks her audiences to venture way outside the box of leadership and business to accept that there are many "other" ways to lead and we have to develop new approaches in order to achieve greatness. She uses spiritual tools and guidance to motivate new action. Pam believes the spirit of leadership can promote sustainable change.

For Women:

More than ever, women need a safe, structured space to gain power within organizations and businesses. We need to train our minds to open in order to help create and advance opportunities for women. The Female Form of Leadership, speaking and training, has a goal to facilitate a shift in mindset, emotion and action around how we value and embrace our confidence as leaders.

Pam's speaking will upgrade how women perceive success, and the Female POD provides a space to look deeply into our beliefs about valuing female leadership can help women break through patterns that hold us back from success.

Spirit:

Pam will motivate your group to fully transform belief systems and take down walls around access to authentic leadership. She will demonstrate that the female form of leadership is a fast path to success and can change stuck systems into successful momentum. Her leadership system is designed to bridge the gaps in leadership so that businesses can experience synergistic growth.

You Do Not have to be a female only team to invite Pam to speak. Pam has a dynamic way about her speaking that is all inclusive and integrative, her goal is to bridge the gap and teach all people to lead from female intuition, creativity and collaboration. Pam will teach to co-ed audiences about the power of everyone accessing leadership despite title, credentials, or position.

Pam's interactive sessions range from 1 hour keynote to one-two day workshops, and offer a new cutting edge way to look at leadership and achieving excellence.

Contact Pam Denton for more information.

Email: drpamdenton@gmail.com
www.PamDenton.com

Advanced Energy Training

~◌⨳◌~

Pam's **Advanced Energy Training** is available for you to train intensively in the science and application of healing the body through channeling universal energy. This intensive practitioner level training will help you understand the transformative effect of increasing energy flow through the body for health, life and prosperity.

Study the power of universal energy, channeling, visualized meditation, soamtic breath-work, spiritual messages and medium communication.

Dr. Pam's **Level 2 Advanced Energy Training**, called **Heart Energy Release (HER)**, is an intensive study of energy medicine, channeling, medium power, spiritual messages and the heart center. It is a deeper journey, entraining the heart center to open, expand and lead. All meditations and energy flow will be directed toward opening the heart center in order to sustain a connection with the emotion of love.

In the AET program, you will study as a practitioner of spiritual channeling and energy healing. Both trainings can be used for hands on healers, doctors, coaches, spiritual guides, energy practitioners and intuitive healers.

The goal of the work is to flush out negative interference and past programming from the soul to create the space for loving consciousness. Join us and begin your journey to heart centered leadership through the power of energy.

To learn more about Dr. Pam and her services go to **www.PamDenton.com**.

51499033R00104

Made in the USA
Middletown, DE
12 November 2017